The Three Ecologies

The Beginning of Knowledge, Hans-Georg Gadamer
The Beginning of Philosophy, Hans-Georg Gadamer
Truth and Method, Hans-Georg Gadamer
All Men Are Brothers, Mohandas K. Gandhi
Things Hidden Since the Foundation of the World, René Girard
Violence and the Sacred, René Girard
Among the Dead Cities, A.C. Grayling
Towards the Light, A.C. Grayling
The Three Ecologies, Félix Guattari
Mindfulness, Martin Heidegger
The Essence of Truth, Martin Heidegger
The Odyssey, Homer
Eclipse of Reason, Max Horkheimer
The Nazi Dictatorship, Ian Kershaw
Language of the Third Reich, Victor Klemperer
Everyday Life in the Modern World, Henri Lefebvre
Rhythmanalysis, Henri Lefebvre
Modes of Modern Writing, David Lodge
Libidinal Economy, Jean-François Lyotard
After Virtue, Alasdair MacIntyre
Time for Revolution, Antonio Negri
Apologia Pro Vita Sua, John Henry Newman
Film Fables, Jacques Rancière
The Politics of Aesthetics, Jacques Rancière
Course in General Linguistics, Ferdinand de Saussure
Philosophy, Roger Scruton
Understanding Music, Roger Scruton
The Five Senses, Michel Serres
The Precariat, Guy Standing
An Actor Prepares, Constantin Stanislavski
Building A Character, Constantin Stanislavski
Creating A Role, Constantin Stanislavski
My Life In Art, Constantin Stanislavski
States and Markets, Susan Strange
What is Art?, Leo Tolstoy
Interrogating the Real, Slavoj Žižek
The Universal Exception, Slavoj Žižek

Some titles are not available in North America.

The Three Ecologies

Félix Guattari

Translated by Ian Pindar and Paul Sutton

BLOOMSBURY ACADEMIC
LONDON • NEW YORK • OXFORD • NEW DELHI • SYDNEY

BLOOMSBURY ACADEMIC
Bloomsbury Publishing Plc
50 Bedford Square, London, WC1B 3DP, UK
1385 Broadway, New York, NY 10018, USA
29 Earlsfort Terrace, Dublin 2, Ireland

BLOOMSBURY, BLOOMSBURY ACADEMIC and the Diana logo are trademarks
of Bloomsbury Publishing Plc

English translation first published in 2000 by The Athlone Press

First published in France 1989

This *Bloomsbury Revelations* edition first published in 2014
by Bloomsbury Academic
Reprinted 2014, 2017, 2018 (twice), 2019, 2020, 2021, 2022, 2023

A catalogue record for this book is available from the British Library.

Guattari, Félix, 1930-1992.
[Trois Ecologies. English]
The three ecologies / Félix Guattari; translated by Ian Pindar and Paul Sutton.
pages cm – (Bloomsbury revelations)
ISBN 978-1-4725-2381-5 (paperback) – ISBN 978-1-4725-3481-1 (epub) –
ISBN 978-1-4725-2825-4 (epdf) 1. Human ecology–Philosophy. I. Title.
GF21.G8313 2014
304.201–dc23
2013050032

ISBN: PB: 978-1-4725-2381-5
ePDF: 978-1-4725-2825-4
ePUB: 978-1-4725-3481-1

Series: Bloomsbury Revelations

Typeset by Newgen Knowledge Works (P) Ltd., Chennai, India
Printed and bound in Great Britain

To find out more about our authors and books visit www.bloomsbury.com
and sign up for our newsletters.

This translation is dedicated to the memory of
Antonella Teresa Sutton (1965–2013)

Contents

Félix Guattari: A Chronology

30 April 1930: Born Pierre-Félix Guattari, he grows up in Villeneuve-les-Sablons, a working-class suburb of north-west Paris.

1940s: Participates in the youth hostelling movement; studies pharmacy and philosophy, and comes into contact with Fernand Oury (1920–98), who would later elaborate institutional pedagogy, which is still taught at Nanterre and survives in organizations such as Association vers la pédagogie institutionnelle.

1950s: Joins the Union des Jeunesses Républicaines de France (UJRF), the youth wing of the Communist Party, but soon forms alliances with various gauchiste dissidents and is eventually suspended. Works with the Parti Communiste Français (PCF), assisting in the publication of the newspaper *Tribune de discussion*.

1953: Becomes involved in establishing La Borde – an experimental psychiatric clinic at the Château de la Borde in the Loir-et-cher in Cour Cheverny, south of Paris – under the directorship of Lacanian analyst Dr Jean Oury (*b*. 1924), brother of Fernand. Guattari had first met Jean Oury in 1945 when he was 15, and at 20 he adopted him as his mentor. La Borde was inspired by the experimental hospital opened in 1940 by François Tosquelles, who rejected the prison camp-like structure of psychiatric institutions. The aim of La Borde was to abolish doctor–patient stereotypes in favour of an interactive group dynamic. In *Chaosmosis* Guattari describes La Borde as a privileged site for social and mental ecology: 'Everything there is set up so that psychotic patients live in a climate of activity and assume responsibility, not only with the goal of developing an ambience of communication, but also in order to create local centres for collective subjectification.' That same year, Jacques Lacan and others form the Société française de Psychanalyse (SFP), after breaking with the Institut de Psychanalyse.

1958: Breaks with the PCF and begins editing and contributing to the dissident newspaper *La Voie communiste*, whose frequent articles in support of Algerian independence lead to its repeated seizure and the imprisonment of two of its directors.

1960s: Active as a technical counsellor in the Mutuelle Nationale d'Etudiants (MNE), the national insurance programme for students; is also involved in the formation of the Groupe de travail de psychologie et de sociologie institutionnelle (GTPSI).

1962: Begins training analysis with Lacan, which lasts for seven years.

1963: The SFP collapses and Lacan and his followers found the École freudienne de Paris.

1965: *La Voie communiste* ceases publication. Guattari founds the Societé de psychothérapie institutionnelle (SPI), which is larger than the GTPSI. He also founds the Fédération des groupes d'études et de recherches institutionnelles (FGERI), an alliance of 300 psychiatrists, psychologists, teachers, town-planners, architects, economists, film-makers, academics and others, dedicated to a general analysis of institutional forms of repression. The FGERI gives birth to the Centre d'étude, de recherche et de formation institutionnelles (CERFI), which publishes the interdisciplinary journal *Recherches*, founded by Guattari in order to 'diversify and radicalize the Left'. The first edition appears in January 1966. He will edit it for the next ten years. He also becomes active in the Opposition de Gauche (OG), an alliance of non-Party gauchistes.

1968, May: *Les événements*. Nine million workers go on strike; students seize the Sorbonne; factories are occupied by workers, lycées by pupils. Students and intellectuals call for a new political order and new forms of social relations free from exploitation and domination – the PCF supports the government. Violent clashes with the police and the army. ('I felt uncomfortable during the street fighting; I was inhibited in terms of physical confrontation with the police.') The FGERI plays a role in the events, notably the occupation of the Théâtre de l'Odeon, where the principles of the 'revolution' are dramatically debated for several days. Guattari sees May 1968 as 'perhaps the last revolution in the old style' and the harbinger of what he calls 'molecular revolution'. 'We were carried along by events, the slogans that were coined, and the splinter groups. But as the song says, "*Je ne regrette rien*"! I learned more things in two months than in twenty years.' His attention shifts to global and international issues, feminism and queer politics.

1969: Becomes an analyst at the École freudienne and remains a member until its dissolution in 1982. He also continues his clinical work at La Borde and starts to build up a psychoanalytic practice. He meets Gilles Deleuze (1925–95), a professor at the new Université de Paris VIII-Vincennes. They correspond, then meet for long conversations and eventually decide to write something together. As Deleuze says: 'We were only two, but what was important for us was less our working together than this strange fact of working between the two of us. We stopped being "author".'

1970s: Forms links with the 'autonomist' groups in France and Italy. He becomes associated in the French press with the autonomist militants, notably through his close friendship with and support of Toni Negri, a former philosophy teacher at the École Normale Supérieure.

1972: *Psychanalyse et transversalité: essais d'analyse institutionnelle* [*Psychoanalysis and Transversality: Essays in Institutional Analysis*] (2nd edn: Preface by Gilles Deleuze). With Gilles Deleuze: *L'anti-Œdipe: capitalisme et schizophrénie I* (*Anti-Oedipus: Capitalism and Schizophrenia I*, 1984).

1973, March/April: Tried and fined 600 francs for committing an 'outrage to public decency' by publishing an issue of *Recherches* (no. 12) entitled 'Trois milliards de pervers, grande encyclopédie des homosexualités' ['Three Billion Perverts: The Great Encyclopedia of Homosexualities']. The issue is described in court as a 'detailed display of depravities and sexual deviations' and the 'libidinous outpourings of a perverted minority'. All copies are ordered to be destroyed. Guattari writes in his notes for the trial: 'Is it really dangerous to let people speak of things as they feel them, and with their language, their passion, their excesses?' He never pays the fine.

1975: With Gilles Deleuze: *Kafka: pour une littérature mineure* (*Kafka: Toward a Minor Literature*, 1986). Helps found and becomes an active member of the Réseau International d'Alternative á la Psychiatrie, an international collective of psychiatrists, nurses and psychiatric patients, with the aim of radically transforming approaches to mental illness. He also becomes President of the Collectif de Soutien aux Radios Libres, which he runs from his apartment, and works with Radio Alice in Bologna, a 'popular free radio' campaign: 'This daily guerrilla warfare of the airwaves . . . the establishment of a veritable feed-back system between the auditors and the broadcast team: whether through direct intervention by phone, through opening "studio" doors, through interviews or programmes based on listener-made cassettes, etc. The Italian experience . . . shows us the immense field of new possibilities that is opened up in this way.'

1977: *La révolution moléculaire* (*Molecular Revolution*: *Psychiatry and Politics*, 1984); Guattari signs 'L'appel des intellectuals français contre le répression en Italie' as a response to the Italian government's repression of the Red Brigade. Other signatories include Gilles Deleuze, Michel Foucault, Philippe Sollers, Roland Barthes and Jean-Paul Sartre.

1979: Toni Negri is arrested for his alleged involvement in terrorist crimes and Guattari publicly supports his friend; *L'Inconscient machinique: essais de schizo-analyse* [*The Machinic Unconscious*: *Essays in Schizoanalysis*]; Guattari founds the Centre d'initiatives pour de nouveaux espaces de liberté (CINEL).

1980: With Gilles Deleuze: *Mille plateaux: capitalisme et schizophrénie II* (*A Thousand Plateaus: Capitalism and Schizophrenia II*, 1988).

1983: Works with Yasha David, a Czech intellectual and refugee, on several large exhibits at the Centre Pompidou, Paris, to commemorate the centenary of Kafka's birth.

1985: With Toni Negri: *Nouvelles espaces de liberté* (*Communists Like Us*, 1990).

1986: *Les années d'hiver 1980–1985* [*The Winter Years 1980–1985*]: 'I come from the ranks of those who lived the 1960s as though it were an interminable spring; so I also experienced some pain in accustoming myself to the long winter of the 1980s.'

1987: Founds the journal *Chiméres* with Gilles Deleuze.

1989: *Les trois écologies* (*The Three Ecologies*, 2000); *Cartographies schizoanalytiques* [*Schizoanalytic Cartographies*].

1991: With Gilles Deleuze: *Qu'est-ce que la philosophie?* (*What is Philosophy?*, 1994); Guattari visits Quebec to attend Oralités, a performance poetry festival organized by his friend J.-J. Lebel.

1992: Stands, unsuccessfully, as a candidate in Paris regional elections, positioning himself between Les Verts (est. 1984) and Génération Écologie (est. 1990): 'The ecological "movement" has nothing to do with quarrels around the leadership of Antoine Waechter and Brice Lalonde. It sets up relays, through dialogue and action, and respects the plurality and diversity of its components. It would be unfortunate if, during the regional elections, which could witness a real groundswell in the ecological vote, Les Verts and Génération Écologie failed to propose common lists of candidates as a first step towards a general recomposition of the ecological movement' ('Une autre vision du futur', *Le Monde*, 15 February); *Chaosmose* (*Chaosmosis*: *An Ethico-aesthetic Paradigm*, 1995); Guattari participates in the Assemblée des citoyens and signs an appeal against the practice of 'ethnic cleansing' in the former Yugoslavia; 29 August: Guattari dies suddenly of a heart attack at the La Borde clinic, aged 62. 'The next day, in the main room, the patients [*fous*] cried when O[ury] told them of Félix's death. "Thank you for telling us like that," they said. That night, in return, even though many of them wandered around, unable to sleep, they had the politeness, the tenderness, not to make any noise. The night was still.' (Depussé, 1993: 145)

Translators' Introduction

HAMM: Nature has forgotten us.

CLOV: There's no more nature.

ENDGAME

In the third plateau of *A Thousand Plateaus* – given the punning title 'The Geology of Morals (Who Does the Earth Think It Is?)' – Félix Guattari and his co-author Gilles Deleuze steal the character of Professor Challenger from Sir Arthur Conan Doyle and have him deliver a lecture in which he argues that the Earth is a body without organs.[1] The Professor Challenger of *A Thousand Plateaus* is, of course, a comic amalgam of Guattari and Deleuze. He is the closest they ever came to a fictional persona and the fun they had with him is apparent, but their Professor is nothing like Conan Doyle's.

When he gave the world Professor Challenger, Conan Doyle was already justly famous for creating Sherlock Holmes. He wrote his two Challenger collections – early examples of a new genre that eventually would be called 'science fiction' – at the turn of the twentieth century: *The Lost World* in 1912 and *The Poison Belt* the following year. Unlike Sherlock Holmes, however, Challenger is almost completely forgotten, although the stereotype he embodied continues to subsist in books, television and film. He is rational, scientific man at the dawn of a new century, confident of his superiority over nature, which is ably demonstrated in the story to which Guattari and Deleuze allude: 'When the Earth Screamed'. Challenger has all the arrogance of Sherlock Holmes but none of his charm. He takes an almost sadistic delight in experimenting on the natural world and despises his much abused,

Watson-like stooge Edward Malone and anyone else who dares to question his superior intelligence ('Clearly a typical victim of the Jehovah complex', observes one of his critics).[2] He is a caricature, of course, but it would not be far-fetched to say that the twentieth century was the century of men like Challenger.

In 'When the Earth Screamed' Challenger argues that the Earth is an organism, much like a sea-urchin, hard on the outside but soft inside. Human beings are a fungal growth of which the planet is completely unaware. Surrounded by sceptics, he proposes to prove his point by vigorously stimulating the creature's sensory cortex, that is, driving a shaft into the centre of the Earth, thereby gaining its attention (for his experiments are always little more than outlets for his insufferable egotism). Having, he supposes, proven his superiority over the rest of animal- and humankind, the Earth is his final and finest challenge: 'I propose to let the Earth know that there is at least one person, George Edward Challenger, who calls for attention – who, indeed, insists upon attention.'

After a brief lecture to a restless audience, Challenger presses the 'electric button' that sends an enormous iron dart into 'the nerve ganglion of old Mother Earth'. There is

> the most horrible yell that ever was heard . . . a howl in which pain, anger, menace, and the outraged majesty of Nature all blended into one hideous shriek. For a full minute it lasted, a thousand sirens in one, paralysing all the great multitude with its fierce insistence, and floating away through the still summer air until it went echoing along the whole south coast and even reached our French neighbours across the Channel. No sound in history has ever equalled the cry of the injured Earth.

Much to Challenger's satisfaction, an 'enormous spout of a vile treacly substance of the consistency of tar' erupts from the ground to soak the assembled Press, and then the excavation is buried by a 50-foot pyramid of earth.

The story ends with Challenger's transformation from lunatic to genius – 'Challenger the super scientist, Challenger the arch-pioneer, Challenger the first man of all men whom Mother Earth had been compelled to recognize' – although it remains unclear what practical benefit the experiment had other than to gratify his terrifying ego or to demonstrate that nothing can 'defend Mother Earth from intrusive Challengers'.

In *The Three Ecologies* Guattari objects that we have challenged the Earth enough and are now on the brink of ecocide. After a century of unparalleled scientific and technological progress we have made our presence known to the planet in the most dramatic and self-defeating fashion. Had the Earth's response to man's 'stimulation' been as localized as it is in Conan Doyle's story – a retaliatory spurt of black tar – we would be safe; but instead we are faced with a very different kind of 'feedback': a bewilderingly complex array of interrelated and unpredictably erratic fluctuations over which we have little or no control and which remind us that the whole world is a giant ecosystem with a sensitive biosphere that has taken 4.5 billion years to evolve.

Our Challenger-like contempt for nature has driven thousands of species to extinction already, insects, other invertebrates and micro-organisms in the main, although birds and larger mammals such as the elephant and the tiger are also at risk, and it is not fanciful to suppose that eventually we might deprive even ourselves of an ecological niche.[3] The Earth's environment is composed of a multiplicity of such niches, each of which is a potential home for life forms. (As Guattari reminds us, the etymology of 'eco' is the Greek word *oïkos*, meaning 'home'.) We have upset the delicate symbiosis between ourselves and nature, with largely unforeseeable results.

In the oceans, for instance, overfishing, increased pollution and rising temperatures as a result of human activity have resulted in the spread of unknown or unidentified infectious 'agents' that have led to the mass mortality of fish, sea mammals, tropical corals and sea-water plants. The biodiversity of the oceans is seriously threatened by mysterious pathogens – viruses, bacteria, fungi and other parasites – that wipe out whole populations. These pathogens are making cross-species leaps of the sort that the Professor Challenger of *A Thousand Plateaus* would be better able to explain, and have exploded the popular belief that the Earth's oceans are so vast they would remain relatively immune from mankind's influence. Whereas Nietzsche could still find comfort in the analogy of the world as a 'sea of forces' that never expends itself, 'eternally flooding back' ('the sea will cast it up again'), we can have no such faith in our diseased and toxic oceans with their oil slicks and giant algae blooms visible from space.[4] There can be little doubt that around the world increased pollution, global warming, deforestation, desertification and the loss of biodiversity are anthropogenic, or that the motor of this generalized impoverishment of the biosphere is capitalism.

The latter half of the twentieth century was a period of intense globalization. With the end of the Cold War and the collapse of the Soviet Union, the dominant mode of economic interaction and transaction was the capitalist system, with its emphasis on the free market. This ideology of unrestricted competition has resulted in the widespread plunder of natural resources, particularly fossil fuels such as oil or coal, but it isn't just the natural environment that is threatened. Poorer countries are forced to sell their labour extremely cheaply in order to enter the global marketplace, and have exploited their natural resources without a thought for sustainability. Meanwhile in the pollution-choked cities of the developed world the most vulnerable in society are living increasingly insecure and alienated lives. Globalization has given rise to 'exploitative practices that perpetuate a quiet violence on low-income labour and other vulnerable groups such as the poor, women and children'.[5] New technological and scientific advances that could be used to liberate human potential remain instead in the service of a capitalist drive for profitability. A third of the world's population continues to suffer from massive poverty and malnutrition, while at the same time there has been an increase in global wealth unprecedented in the history of humankind.

The increasing globalization of all areas of our lives is not being directed by one particular capitalist organization, party or country – not even the USA, despite the fact that the model which most of the world is confronted with is the American Way of Life. Post-industrial capitalism – which Guattari calls Integrated World Capitalism (IWC) – is delocalized and deterritorialized to such an extent that it is impossible to locate the source of its power.[6] IWC's most potent weapon for achieving social control without violence is the mass media. For instance, everyone nowadays has a television set. Many people in the Third World will have televisions long before they have proper irrigation. With the worldwide domination of capitalism came a parallel expansion in communications technology. Instant global communication became a reality leading to the creation of a 'global village': the world as a single community linked by telecommunications. The mass media is involved in the creation of demand, so there will always be a market for capital investment.[7] A new type of individual is being shaped and moulded by the unseen pressure of market forces.

In *The Three Ecologies* Guattari argues that we are being 'mentally manipulated through the production of a collective, mass-media subjectivity'. That there might be a need for a *mental ecology* is one of the most profound ideas in this short book. Guattari's contention is that IWC is not only destroying the natural environment and eroding social relations, but is also engaged in a far more insidious and invisible 'penetration of people's attitudes, sensibility and minds' (Guattari and Negri, 1990: 53). Human subjectivity, in all its uniqueness – what Guattari calls its 'singularity' – is as endangered as those rare species that are disappearing from the planet every day. It is up to us to resist this mass-media homogenization, which is both desingularizing and infantalizing, and instead invent new ways to achieve the resingularization of existence. It is not enough to take to the streets and wave placards, an entire mental ecology is necessary in order not to give IWC our *unconscious* assent. But to illustrate how IWC infiltrates and saturates the unconscious, let us return briefly to its effect on the environment.

It might have been better for us if the Earth had screamed, as it did for Professor Challenger. Instead it has gone eerily silent. Take, for example, the population of songbirds in the British countryside. In 1972 there were an estimated 7.72 million skylarks in Britain. By 1996 there were only about 3.09 million. In a short space of time almost 60 per cent had disappeared.[8] It is very rare to hear a skylark today, as it is to hear other once common songbirds such as the song thrush or the blackbird. Their ecological niches or homes – hedgerows, heaths, ponds, meadows, moors and marshes – have been eroded by the intensive use of agri-chemicals and pesticides which have decimated their food supply. Birds sing to mark out their territory (Deleuze and Guattari, 1988: 312), so it is only to be expected that the singing has stopped.

It is a sound that Thomas Hardy, in another century, could take for granted: 'the voice of a weak bird singing a trite old evening song that might doubtless have been heard on the hill at the same hour, and with the selfsame trills, quavers, and breves . . . for centuries untold' (Hardy, 1987: 71). Guattari calls this conjunction of a recognizable melodic formula and a territory a 'refrain', and 'the simplest examples of refrains delimiting existential Territories can be found in the ethology of numerous bird species' (1995a: 15).

There are many refrains in our own lives as well, a favourite song, the advertising jingle that we can't get out of our heads, even singing to the radio, for radio and television sets create 'sound walls' around us (Deleuze and Guattari, 1988: 311). In *The Three Ecologies* Guattari argues that 'Individuals are "captured" by their environment, by ideas, tastes, models, ways of being, the images that are constantly injected into them, and even by the refrains that go round and round in their heads'. In fact, surrounded by all these different refrains which pass through us, it is difficult to know where, or rather, who 'we' are, especially when the most dominant refrains are provided by IWC's ideological arm, the mass media.

The machinic enslavement of television is a good example. Do we really use television or does it use us? Are we not in danger of becoming intrinsic component pieces in a much larger machine? (Deleuze and Guattari, 1988: 458). As Guattari remarks in *Chaosmosis*:

When I watch television, I exist at the intersection: (1) of a perceptual fascination provoked by the screen's luminous animation which borders on the hypnotic; (2) of a captive relation with the narrative content of the programme, associated with a lateral awareness of surrounding events (water boiling on the stove, a child's cry, the telephone . . .); (3) of a world of phantasms occupying my daydreams. My feeling of personal identity is thus pulled in different directions. How can I maintain a relative sense of unicity, despite the diversity of components of subjectification that pass through me? It's a question of the refrain that fixes me in front of the screen. (1995a: 16–17)

IWC seeks to gain power over us by 'controlling and neutralizing the maximum number of existential refrains', thereby determining the limits within which we think, feel and live; a process of 'existential contraction'. We don't get out much; we tend to think what everyone else thinks, feel the same as everyone else; a strange passivity haunts our lives.[9] As market-driven technologies provide new, ever more effective means of modifying our subjectivity at deeper and deeper levels, we are becoming more homogenized. The world is shrinking, and so are we. 'A vast majority of individuals are placed in a situation in which their personality is dwindling, their intentions are rapidly losing all consistency, the quality of their relations with others is dulled' (Guattari, 1989c: 19). For Guattari, 'consistency' is indissociable from heterogeneity, and much of *The Three Ecologies* is concerned with attaining consistency again, becoming heterogeneous, resingularizing ourselves, affirming our legitimate difference both from each other and from a notional 'Self'.

It is a question of making a pragmatic intervention in one's own life in order to escape from the dominant capitalistic subjectivity. The objective of the new ecological practices that Guattari outlines is to 'activate isolated and repressed singularities that are turning around on themselves'. It isn't a question of exchanging one model or way of life for another, but of 'respond[ing] to the event as the potential bearer of new constellations of Universes of reference' (1995a: 18). The paradox is this: although these Universes are not pre-established reference points or models, with their discovery one realizes they were always already there, but only a singular event could activate them.

In *Chaosmosis*, Guattari uses the example of a patient who is stuck in a rut, going round and round in circles. One day, on the spur of the moment, he decides to take up driving again. As he does so he immediately activates an existentializing refrain that opens up 'new fields of virtuality' for him. He renews contact with old friends, drives to familiar spots and regains his self-confidence (1995a: 17). This is what Guattari calls 'a processual exploitation of event-centred "singularities"' (1995a: 7). It is notable that Guattari seems to have experienced something similar when he learned to drive at the comparatively late age of 35. His life changed dramatically when he got his driving licence: 'I became more independent, which eventually led, among other things, to a divorce' (1996a: 241; 1989a: 244).

Guattari's favourite – Proustian – example of an existentializing refrain is the effect on Swann of the 'little phrase' from the Vinteuil sonata. This refrain has 'a sort of *re-creative* influence' upon Swann; he is 'like a confirmed invalid in whom, all of a sudden, a change of air and surroundings, or a new course of treatment, or sometimes an organic change in himself, *spontaneous and unaccountable*, seems to have brought about such an improvement in his health that he begins to envisage the possibility, hitherto beyond all hope, of starting to lead belatedly a wholly different life'.[10] An existential Territory can either become stratified and trapped in 'deathly repetitions', as in the case of the tele-spectator in front of the screen watching advertisements, or is capable of being reactivated by a singular event, as in the case of the patient who takes up driving.

The idea of a singular event in one's life, which may be almost imperceptible but which has enormous repercussions, is borrowed from modern physics. It was apparent to the physicist James Clerk Maxwell as long ago as the nineteenth century that singular events or points might have a political – or what Guattari would call micropolitical – application and a catalysing power:

> the system has a quantity of potential energy, which is capable of being transformed into motion, but which cannot begin to be so transformed till the system has reached a certain configuration, to attain which requires *an expenditure of work*, which in certain cases may be infinitesimally small, and in general bears no definite proportion to the energy developed in consequence thereof. For example, a rock loosed by frost and balanced on a singular point of the mountain-side, the little spark which kindles the great forest, the little word which sets the world a-fighting, the little scruple which prevents a man from doing his will, the little spore which blights all the potatoes, the little gemmule which makes us philosophers or idiots. Every existence above a certain rank has its singular points: the higher the rank, the more of them. At these points, influences *whose physical magnitude is too small to be taken account of by a finite being*, may produce results of the greatest importance. All great

results produced by human endeavour depend on taking advantage of these singular points when they occur.[11]

Guattari is fascinated by the non-human aspect of subjectivity. Singularity is not individuality, although it is about being singular. It operates at a pre-personal, pre-individual level. In *The Three Ecologies* he compares our interior life or 'interiority' to a crossroads where several components of subjectification meet to make up who we think we are. The resingularization of subjectivity, the liberation of singularities that are repressed by a dominant and dominating mass-media subjectivity, has nothing to do with individuals.[12]

Nevertheless, an expenditure of work is necessary in order for us to extend our existential Territories. One of the most insistent refrains in *The Three Ecologies* is that we must abandon scientific (or pseudo-scientific) paradigms and return to aesthetic ones. We need to continually reinvent our lives like an artist. 'Life', as Guattari has said elsewhere, 'is like a performance, one must construct it, work at it, singularize it' (1989c: 20). It is an ongoing aesthetico-existential process. 'As we . . . weave and unweave our bodies . . . from day to day, their molecules shuttled to and fro, so does the artist weave and unweave his image' (Joyce, 1986: 159). In *The Three Ecologies* it is artists who provide us with the most profound insights into the human condition, not professional scientists or psychoanalysts. Goethe, Proust, Joyce, Artaud and Beckett are all cited, but there are many others. Büchner, for example, whose *Lenz* is a classic study in schizophrenia long before the term was invented and has been described as 'proof that poetic utterances can anticipate scientific advances by decades',[13] or Sacher-Masoch, whose *Venus in Furs* diagnosed an entire condition to which he reluctantly gave his name.[14]

The best artists don't repeat themselves, they start over and over again from scratch, uncertain with each new attempt precisely where their next experiment will take them, but then suddenly, spontaneously and unaccountably, as the painter Francis Bacon has observed, 'there comes something which your instinct seizes on as being for a moment the thing which you could begin to develop'.[15] Life is a work in progress, with no goal in sight, only the tireless endeavour to explore new possibilities, to respond to the chance event – the singular point – that takes us off in a new direction. As Bacon once remarked, 'I always think of myself not so much as a painter but as a medium for accident and chance.'[16]

So, Guattari has extended his definition of ecology beyond merely environmental concerns to include human subjectivity itself, but what about social relations? It is all very well for people to become mental ecologists, to live their lives like a work of art in a state of pure, creative autoreferentiality, but the question arises as to how they can then work together, collectively, in a unified struggle against IWC's damaging effect on society. Is it not the case that processes of singularization that actively multiply differences make any mass movement impossible?

People are not yet as pacified and domesticated as IWC would like them to be. As early as 1977, Guattari observed that 'ever-widening social groups are not content to go on as they always have. An increasing number of people are beginning to reject certain forms of consumerism. To exhortations to acquire more cars, more private houses, more household machines, more ready-made entertainment and, in order to do so, to work harder, join the rat race, wear oneself out before one's time, they reply, "What's the point? Who does it help?"' (1984: 251). These people obviously share a similar sense of alienation from the capitalist consensus, but how can they act collectively to alter their circumstances? 'Rather than looking for a stupefying and infantalizing consensus', he proposes in *The Three Ecologies*, 'it will be a question in the future of cultivating a *dissensus*.'

Guattari's finely nuanced, radically dissensual approach to *social ecology* requires the collective production of unpredictable and untamed 'dissident subjectivities' rather than a mass movement of like-minded people.

> Work on oneself, in as much as one is a collective singularity; construct and in a permanent way re-construct this collectivity in a multivalent liberation project. Not in reference to a directing ideology, but within the articulations of the Real. Perpetually recomposing subjectivity and praxis is only conceivable in the totally free movement of each of its components, and in absolute respect of their own times – time for comprehending or refusing to comprehend, time to be unified or

to be autonomous, time of identification or of the most exacerbated differences. (Guattari and Negri, 1990: 120)

As he makes clear in *The Three Ecologies*, there will be moments when eco-activists work together, and other times when they drift apart again. The important thing is that they do not have a leader directing their activity.[17] *The Three Ecologies* was written before the Internet had fully developed into the powerful recruitment tool it is today, but Guattari was not unaware of the 'proliferation of spontaneous and co-ordinated groups' using the more rudimentary French Minitel system.[18] It is one instance in which technological advancements may work for the collective good, leading to globally organized autonomous action and short-lived but effective affinity groups in which 'the intensity of the minority's feelings can be revealed to the majority by the minority engaging in civil disobedience' (Carter, 1999: 258). Dissensus is principally a call for the revival of individual competence as a social force, for the development of new, 'egalitarian, decentralized, participatory democracies, orientated towards an environmentally sustainable way of living' (Carter, 1999: 300).

There is of course a tension at work here between solidarity and dissensus. It requires that a plurality of disparate groups come together in a kind of unified disunity, a pragmatic solidarity without solidity; what one might call, for want of a better word, 'fluidarity'. The common enemy – IWC – has become so ubiquitous, and its deleterious effect on the planet so apparent, that no strata of society is immune from its effects. This is what makes ecology – or ecosophy – such a potentially radical force in the world. We are all of us prey to environmental degradation, we are all stranded on Spaceship Earth.

A capitalism that does not exploit resources – be they natural or human – is as yet unthinkable. A capitalism that is symbiotic rather than parasitic may never be possible. As Gregory Bateson points out, for too long humanity has adopted 'survival of the fittest' as its maxim – and this is taken to its extreme by free-market competition – whereas if humanity is to survive it must reconfigure this goal into that of 'survival of organism plus environment' (Bateson, 1972: 499). At present the major capitalist countries are also the major polluters of the Earth. The mass media creates a climate of unquestioning passivity. The role of television in perpetuating the perception that 'environmental problems' occur in some ill-defined elsewhere can only work in IWC's interest.[19] But even if governments and industry acted immediately to reduce the global emission of greenhouse gases, for instance, it would still take hundreds of years for the Earth's ecological equilibrium to be restored. Unfortunately, immediate political action is unlikely when the worst polluting nations continue to insist that 'emissions trading' occurs under free-market principles.

From a cosmic perspective the human race is at the beginning of the evolutionary process. There is time for life to spread beyond the Earth throughout the entire Cosmos, provided the planet's biosphere isn't destroyed. While it is trapped on Spaceship Earth, and now that it has entered the nuclear and biotechnological age, our species remains vulnerable. In order for it to survive, the twenty-first century must be atheist in the best sense: a positive disbelief in God, concerned only with, and respectful of, *terrestrial* life. It will require the development of an immanent, materialist ethics, coupled with an atheist awareness of finitude, of the mortality of the species, the planet and the entire universe, and not an illusory belief in immortality, which is only a misplaced contempt for life.[20] A proper understanding of our terrestriality and mortality does not imply any restriction of our horizons. There will always be new ways of life to be invented, for there are as many different ways of living as there are people; provided we rediscover our heterogeneity and resist the insidious normalization of our lives.

As Bateson has argued (1972: 495–505), an ecological struggle for survival is taking place in the domain of *ideas*. The task of every ecological analyst now is to promote ecologically 'good' ideas in the hope that these will prevail, through a process of natural selection, over ecologically 'bad' ideas that will prove fatal to the planet. *The Three Ecologies* is full of ecologically 'good' ideas. It is a modest proposal that we should protect not only the Earth and society, but also our own rare and singular minds from the encroachments of Integrated World Capitalism.

Guattari has done all he could. The rest is up to natural selection.

Note on the Translation and Acknowledgements

We have sought in this translation to retain the tenor of the original French, including, as far as is possible, Guattari's verbal idiosyncrasies. We have also tried to maintain a terminological consistency with earlier translations of Guattari's works, including those co-authored with Gilles Deleuze. Brian Massumi's masterful translation of *A Thousand Plateaus* has been, in most cases, our lodestar. So *agencement* has been translated as 'assemblage'; *agencement d'énonciation* as 'assemblage of enunciation'; *devenir-femme* as 'becoming-woman' and the same for other becomings; *machine de guerre* as 'war machine'; *mot d'ordre* as 'order-word'; *nationalitaire* as 'nationalitary'; *ritournelle* as 'refrain'; *subjectivation* as 'subjectification'; *visagéitaire* as 'faciality'; all of which decisions are explained in the notes, where other words such as *auto-destruction* and *dispositif* are also discussed. In many previous translations of Guattari's writings, his use of 'etc.' has been expunged, but it seems to us important to retain it in order to make clear that the examples he gives should not be arbitrarily closed off as though they were the only ones, but left open-ended to be added to by those who come after. Nevertheless, we felt that his free use of the exclamation mark, while acceptable in much French writing, might make him sound over-excitable to Anglo-Saxon ears.

The reader will find that many of the notes are ours rather than Guattari's. The original French text of *The Three Ecologies* is very lightly annotated, but it was felt that more explanation was needed for the English reader unfamiliar with Guattari's considerable *oeuvre* and his many neologisms. We have taken care to source his ideas to his published work in English, in the hope that this short book might introduce a new generation of readers to Guattari. In *Chaosmosis*, his last book, Guattari offers us some guidance as to how one should approach his work: 'Just as an artist borrows from his precursors and his contemporaries the traits which suit him, I invite those who read me to take or reject my concepts freely.'

*

We would like to thank all those who have given us advice and assistance during the preparation of this book, including Gary Genosko, Brian Massumi and Jeremy Munday for their invaluable comments on the text, Tristan Palmer, our patient editor, Sarah Andersen, Bruce Bennett, Karen Eliot, Victoria Keams, and finally Antonella Sutton-Smith, without whom none of this would have been possible.

The Three Ecologies

For Sacha Goldman

There is an ecology of bad ideas, just as there is an ecology of weeds.

GREGORY BATESON[1]

The Earth is undergoing a period of intense techno-scientific transformations. If no remedy is found, the ecological disequilibrium this has generated will ultimately threaten the continuation of life on the planet's surface. Alongside these upheavals, human modes of life, both individual and collective, are progressively deteriorating. Kinship networks tend to be reduced to a bare minimum; domestic life is being poisoned by the gangrene of mass-media consumption; family and married life are frequently 'ossified' by a sort of standardization of behaviour; and neighbourhood relations are generally reduced to their meanest expression . . . It is the relationship between subjectivity and its exteriority – be it social, animal, vegetable or Cosmic – that is compromised in this way, in a sort of general movement of implosion and regressive infantalization. Otherness [*l'altérité*] tends to lose all its asperity. Tourism, for example, usually amounts to no more than a journey on the spot, with the same redundancies of images and behaviour.

Political groupings and executive authorities appear to be totally incapable of understanding the full implications of these issues. Despite having recently initiated a partial realization of the most obvious dangers that threaten the natural environment of our societies, they are generally content to simply tackle industrial pollution and then from a purely technocratic perspective, whereas only an ethico-political articulation – which I call *ecosophy* – between the three ecological registers (the environment, social relations and human subjectivity) would be likely to clarify these questions.[2]

Henceforth it is the ways of living on this planet that are in question, in the context of the acceleration of techno-scientific mutations and of considerable demographic growth. Through the continuous development of machinic labour, multiplied by the information revolution, productive forces can make available an increasing amount of time for potential human activity.[3] But to what end? Unemployment, oppressive marginalization, loneliness, boredom, anxiety and neurosis? Or culture, creation, development, the reinvention of the environment and the enrichment of modes of life and sensibility? In both the Third World and the developed world, whole sections of the collective subjectivity are floundering or simply huddle around archaisms; as is the case, for example, with the dreadful rise of religious fundamentalism.[4]

The only true response to the ecological crisis is on a global scale, provided that it brings about an authentic political, social and cultural revolution, reshaping the objectives of the production of both material and immaterial assets. Therefore this revolution must not be exclusively concerned with visible relations of force on a grand scale, but will also take into account molecular domains of sensibility, intelligence and desire. A finalization of social labour, regulated in a univocal way by a profit economy and by power relations, would only lead, at present, to dramatic dead-ends. This is obvious from the absurd and burdensome economic supervisions of the Third World, which lead some of its regions into an absolute and irreversible pauperization. It is equally evident in countries like France, where the proliferation of nuclear power stations threatens, over a large part of Europe, the possible consequences of Chernobyl-style accidents.[5] One need hardly mention the almost delirious stockpiling of thousands of nuclear warheads, which, at the slightest technical or human error, could automatically lead to collective extermination. In all of these examples it is the same dominant modes of valorizing human activities that are implicated. That is to say:

1   those of the imperium [Latin: 'authority'] of a global market that destroys specific value systems and puts on the same plane of equivalence: material assets, cultural assets, wildlife areas, etc.;

2 those that place all social and international relations under the control of police and military machines.

Trapped in this double pincer movement, the nation States see their traditional role of mediation being reduced more and more, and they are frequently put in the combined service of the authorities of the global marketplace and of military–industrial complexes.[6]

The current situation is all the more paradoxical as the time is almost over when the world was placed under the aegis of an East–West antagonism, a largely imaginary projection of working-class/middle-class oppositions within capitalist countries.[7] Does this mean that the new, multipolar issues of the three ecologies will simply take the place of the old class struggles and their myths of reference? Of course, such a substitution will not be automatic! But it nevertheless appears probable that these issues, which correspond to an extreme complexification of social, economic and international contexts, will increasingly come to the foreground.

Initially the class antagonisms that were inherited from the nineteenth century contributed to the creation of homogeneous, bipolarized fields of subjectivity. Then, during the second half of the twentieth century, the hardline worker subjectivity crumbled with the advent of the consumer society, the welfare system, the media, etc. Despite the fact that today these segregations and hierarchies have never been so intensively experienced, this group of subjective positions has been cloaked by the same fictitious smokescreen. A vague sense of social belonging has deprived the old class consciousness of its tension.[8] (I won't go into the accumulation of violently heterogeneous subjective poles, such as those that are emerging in the Muslim world.) For their part, the so-called socialist countries have steadily introjected the 'unidimensionalizing' value systems of the West.[9] Therefore, in the communist world the old facade of egalitarianism is giving way to mass-media serialism (the same ideal standards of living, the same fashions and types of rock music, etc.).[10]

It is difficult to imagine the situation can be improved in any significant way as far as the North–South axis is concerned. Admittedly, in the end, it is conceivable that the spread of agri-business techniques will allow us to modify the theoretical givens of the tragedy of world hunger. But on the ground, meanwhile, it would be a complete illusion to think that international aid, such as it is designed and distributed today, would be able to permanently resolve every problem. Henceforth, the long-term establishment of immense zones of misery, hunger and death seems to play an integral part in the monstrous system of 'stimulation' that is Integrated World Capitalism. In any case, the hyper-exploitative New Industrial Powers, such as Hong Kong, Taiwan, South Korea, etc., depend on these zones for their development.

We find this same principle of social tension and 'stimulation' born of despair in the developed countries, with the establishment of periods of chronic unemployment and the increasing marginalization of the population: the young, the old, 'part-time' workers, the undervalued, etc.

So, wherever we turn, there is the same nagging paradox: on the one hand, the continuous development of new techno-scientific means to potentially resolve the dominant ecological issues and reinstate socially useful activities on the surface of the planet, and, on the other hand, the inability of organized social forces and constituted subjective formations to take hold of these resources in order to make them work.

But perhaps this paroxysmal era of the erosion of subjectivities, assets and environments is destined to enter into a phase of decline. The demands of singularity are rising up almost everywhere; the most obvious signs in this regard are to be found in the multiplication of nationalitary claims which were regarded as marginal only yesterday, and which increasingly occupy the foreground of the political stage.[11] (We note, from Corsica to the Baltic States, the conjunction of ecological and separatist demands.) In the end, this rise in nationalitary questions will probably lead to profound modifications in East–West relations, and in particular, the configuration of Europe, whose centre of gravity could drift decisively towards a neutralist East.

The traditional dualist oppositions that have guided social thought and geopolitical cartographies are over. The conflicts remain, but they engage with multipolar systems incompatible with recruitments under any ideological, Manicheist flag.[12] For example, the opposition between the Third World and the developed world is being completely blown apart. We have seen with the New Industrial Powers that productivity is becoming on an altogether different scale from the traditional industrial bastions of the West, but this phenomenon is accompanied by a sort of Third-Worldization within developed countries, which is coupled with an exacerbation of questions relative to immigration and racism.[13] Make no mistake about it, the great disorder and confusion surrounding the economic unification of the European Community will in no way impede this Third-Worldization of considerable areas of Europe.

Another antagonism, transversal to that of class struggles, remains that of the relations between men and women. On a global scale, the female condition is far from being ameliorated. The exploitation of female labour, like that of child labour, is as bad now as it was in the worst periods of the nineteenth century! Nevertheless, for the last two decades, a gradual subjective revolution has modified the female condition. Although the sexual independence of women is very unequally developed in correlation with the availability of methods of contraception and abortion, and although the rise of religious fundamentalism continues to minorize them, some indices lead us to think that long-term transformations – in Fernand Braudel's sense – are well and truly on the way (the appointment of women as heads of State, demands for equality between men and women at important representative levels, etc.).[14]

As for young people, although they are crushed by the dominant economic relations which make their position increasingly precarious, and although they are mentally manipulated through the production of a collective, mass-media subjectivity, they are nevertheless developing their own methods of distancing themselves from normalized subjectivity through singularization. In this respect, the transnational character of rock music is extremely significant; it plays the role of a sort of initiatory cult, which confers a cultural pseudo-identity on a considerable mass of young people and allows them to obtain for themselves a bare minimum of existential Territories.[15]

It is in this context of break-up and decentralization, the multiplication of antagonisms and processes of singularization, that the new ecological problematics suddenly appear. Don't misunderstand me, I don't claim in the least that they can be relied upon to take charge of the other lines of molecular fracture, but it appears to me that they lead to a problematization that is transversal to them.

If it is no longer a question – as it was in previous periods of class struggle or the defence of the 'fatherland of socialism' – of creating an unequivocal ideology, it is conceivable, on the other hand, that the new ecosophical example indicates the lines of reconstruction of human praxis in the most varied domains.[16] At every level, individual or collective, in everyday life as well as the reinvention of democracy (concerning town planning, artistic creation, sport, etc.), it is a question in each instance of looking into what would be the dispositives of the production of subjectivity, which tends towards an individual and/or collective resingularization, rather than that of mass-media manufacture, which is synonymous with distress and despair.[17] The ecosophical perspective does not totally exclude a definition of unifying objectives, such as the struggle against world hunger, an end to deforestation or to the blind proliferation of the nuclear industries; but it will no longer be a question of depending on reductionist, stereotypical order-words which only expropriate other more singular problematics and lead to the promotion of charismatic leaders.[18]

The same ethico-political aim runs through the questions of racism, of phallocentrism, of the disastrous legacy of a self-congratulatory 'modern' town planning, of an artistic creation liberated from the market system, of an education system able to appoint its own social mediators, etc.[19] In the final account, the ecosophic problematic is that of the production of human existence itself in new historical contexts.

Social ecosophy will consist in developing specific practices that will modify and reinvent the ways in which we live as couples or in the family, in an urban context or at work, etc. Obviously it would be inconceivable to try and go back to the old formulas, which relate to periods when the planet was far less densely populated and when social relations were much stronger than they are today. But it will be a question of literally reconstructing the modalities of 'group-being' [l'êtreen-groupe], not only through 'communicational' interventions but through existential mutations driven by the motor of subjectivity. Instead of clinging to general recommendations we would be implementing effective practices of experimentation, as much on a micro-social level as on a larger institutional scale.

For its part, mental ecosophy will lead us to reinvent the relation of the subject to the body, to phantasm, to the passage of time, to the 'mysteries' of life and death. It will lead us to search for antidotes to mass media and telematic standardization, the conformism of fashion, the manipulation of opinion by advertising, surveys, etc.[20] Its ways of operating will be more like those of an artist, rather than of professional psychiatrists who are always haunted by an outmoded ideal of scientificity.

Nothing in these domains is played out in the name of history, in the name of infrastructural determinisms! Barbaric implosion cannot be entirely ruled out. And, for want of such an ecosophical revival (or whatever we wish to call it), for want of a rearticulation of the three fundamental types of ecology, we can unfortunately predict the rise of all kinds of danger: racism, religious fanaticism, nationalitary schisms that suddenly flip into reactionary closure, the exploitation of child labour, the oppression of women. . .

Let us now try to grasp the implications of such an ecosophical perspective on our conception of subjectivity.

The subject is not a straightforward matter; it is not sufficient to think in order to be, as Descartes declares, since all sorts of other ways of existing have already established themselves outside consciousness, while any mode of thought that desperately tries to gain a hold on itself merely turns round and round like a mad spinning top, without ever attaching itself to the real Territories of existence; which, for their part, drift in relation to each other like tectonic plates under continents.[21] Rather than speak of the 'subject', we should perhaps speak of *components of subjectification*, each working more or less on its own. This would lead us, necessarily, to re-examine the relation between concepts of the individual and subjectivity, and, above all, to make a clear distinction between the two. Vectors of subjectification do not necessarily pass through the individual, which in reality appears to be something like a 'terminal' for processes that involve human groups, socio-economic ensembles, data-processing machines, etc. Therefore, interiority establishes itself at the crossroads of multiple components, each relatively autonomous in relation to the other, and, if need be, in open conflict.

I know that it remains difficult to get people to listen to such arguments, especially in those contexts where there is still a suspicion – or even an automatic rejection – of any specific reference to subjectivity. In the name of the primacy of infrastructures, of structures or systems, subjectivity still gets a bad press, and those who deal with it, in practice or theory, will generally only approach it at arm's length, with infinite precautions, taking care never to move too far away from pseudo-scientific paradigms, preferably borrowed from the hard sciences: thermodynamics, topology, information theory, systems theory, linguistics, etc. It is as though a scientistic superego demands that psychic entities are reified and insists that they are only understood by means of extrinsic coordinates. Under such conditions, it is no surprise that the human and social sciences have condemned themselves to missing the intrinsically progressive, creative and auto-positioning dimensions of processes of subjectification. In this context, it appears crucial to me that we rid ourselves of all scientistic references and metaphors in order to forge new paradigms that are instead ethico-aesthetic in inspiration. Besides, are not the best cartographies of the psyche, or, if you like, the best psychoanalyses, those of Goethe, Proust, Joyce, Artaud and Beckett, rather than Freud, Jung and Lacan? In fact, it is the literary component in the works of the latter that best survives (for example, Freud's *The Interpretation of Dreams* can perhaps be regarded as an extraordinary modern novel!).

My reassessment of psychoanalysis proceeds from a concern with aesthetic creation and with ethical implications, yet it doesn't at all presuppose a 'rehabilitation' of phenomenological analysis, which I consider to be handicapped by a systematic 'reductionism' that leads it to reduce the objects under consideration to a pure intentional transparency. I myself have come to regard the apprehension of a psychical fact as inseparable from the assemblage of enunciation that engenders it, both as fact and as expressive process.[22] There is a kind of relationship of uncertainty between the apprehension [*la saisie*] of the object and the apprehension of the subject; so that, to articulate them both, one is compelled to make a *pseudo-narrative* detour through the annals of myth and ritual or through supposedly scientific accounts [*descriptions*] – all of which have as their ultimate goal a *dis-positional mise en scène*, a bringing-into-existence, that authorizes, 'secondarily', a discursive intelligibility.[23] I am not advocating a return to the Pascalian distinction between the mathematical and the intuitive mind, for these two types of understanding, conceptual on the one hand and affective or perceptive on the other, are in fact entirely complementary.[24] However, I am suggesting that this pseudo-narrative detour deploys repetitions that function, through an infinite variety of rhythms and refrains, as the very supports of existence.[25] Discourse, or any discursive chain, thus becomes the bearer of a non-discursivity which, like a stroboscopic trace, nullifies the play of distinctive oppositions at the level of both content and form of expression.[26] It is only through these repetitions that incorporeal Universes of reference, whose singular events punctuate the progress of individual and collective historicity, can be generated and regenerated.

Just as Greek theatre and courtly love or chivalric romance were once adopted as models or rather as modules of subjectification, so, today it is Freudianism which continues to underwrite our perception of sexuality, childhood, neurosis, etc.[27] I do not at present envisage 'going beyond' Freudianism [*le fait freudien*] or breaking definitively with it, however I do want to reorient Freud's concepts and practices so as to use them differently; I want to uproot them from their pre-structuralist ties, from a subjectivity anchored solidly in the individual and collective past. From now on what will be on the agenda is a 'futurist' and 'constructivist' opening up of the fields of virtuality. The unconscious remains bound to archaic fixations only as long as there is no investment [*engagement*] directing it towards the future. This existential tension will proceed through the bias of human and even non-human temporalities such as the acceleration of the technological and data-processing revolutions, as prefigured in the phenomenal growth of a computer-aided subjectivity, which will lead to the opening up or, if you prefer, the unfolding [*dépliage*], of animal-, vegetable-, Cosmic- and machinic-becomings. At the same time we should not forget that the formation and 'remote-controlling' of human individuals and groups will be governed by institutional and social class dimensions.

In short, the mythic and phantasmatic lure of psychoanalysis must be resisted, it must be played with, rather than cultivated and tended like an ornamental garden![28] Unfortunately, the psychoanalysts of today, more so than their predecessors, take refuge behind what one might call a 'structuralization' of unconscious complexes, which leads to dry theorization and to an insufferable dogmatism; also, their practice ends up impoverishing their treatments and produces a stereotyping which renders them insensible to the singular otherness [*alterité*] of their patients.[29]

I have invoked ethical paradigms principally in order to underline the responsibility and necessary 'engagement' required not only of psychiatrists but also all of those in the fields of education, health, culture, sport, the arts, the media and fashion, who are in a position to intervene in individual and collective psychical proceedings. It is ethically untenable for these psychiatrists to shelter, as they so often do, behind a transferential neutrality supposedly founded upon a scientific corpus and on a perfect mastery of the unconscious. More so given that the domain of psychiatry has established itself as the extension of, and at the interface with, aesthetic domains.

I have stressed these aesthetic paradigms because I want to emphasize that everything, particularly in the field of practical psychiatry, has to be continually reinvented, started again from scratch, otherwise the processes become trapped in a cycle of deathly repetition [*répétition mortifère*]. The precondition for any revival of analysis – through schizoanalysis, for example – consists in accepting that as a general rule, and however little one works on them, individual and collective subjective assemblages are capable, potentially, of developing and proliferating well beyond their ordinary equilibrium.[30] By their very essence analytic cartographies extend beyond the existential Territories to which they are assigned. As in painting or literature, the concrete performance of these cartographies requires that they evolve and innovate, that they open up new futures, without their authors [*auteurs*] having prior recourse to assured theoretical principles or to the authority of a group, a school or an academy . . . Work in progress![31] An end to psychoanalytic, behaviourist or systematist catechisms. In order to converge with the perspective of the art world, psychiatrists must demonstrate that they have abandoned their white coats, beginning with those invisible ones that they wear in their heads, in their language and in the ways they conduct themselves. The goal of a painter is not to repeat the same painting indefinitely (unless they are Titorelli, who in Kafka's *The Trial* always painted identical portraits of the same judge).[32] Similarly, every care organization, or aid agency, every educational institution and any individual course of treatment ought to have as its primary concern the continuous development of its practices as much as its theoretical scaffolding.

Paradoxically, it is perhaps in the 'hard' sciences that we encounter the most spectacular reconsideration of processes of subjectification; Prigogine and Stengers, for example, refer to the necessity of introducing into physics a 'narrative element', which they regard as indispensable for the theorization of evolution in terms of irreversibility.[33] All the same I am convinced that the question of subjective enunciation will pose itself ever more forcefully as machines producing signs, images, syntax and artificial intelligence continue to develop. Here we are talking about a reconstruction of social and individual practices which I shall classify under three complementary headings, all of which come under the ethico-aesthetic aegis of an ecosophy: social ecology, mental ecology and environmental ecology.

The increasing deterioration of human relations with the socius, the psyche and 'nature' is due not only to environmental and objective pollution but is also the result of a certain incomprehension and fatalistic passivity towards these issues as a whole, among both individuals and governments. Catastrophic or not, negative developments [*évolutions*] are simply accepted without question. Structuralism and subsequently post-modernism has accustomed us to a vision of the world drained of the significance of human interventions, embodied as they are in concrete politics and micropolitics.[34] The explanations offered for this decline of social praxes – the death of ideologies and the return to universal values – seem to me unsatisfactory. Rather, it appears to be a result of the failure of social and psychological praxes to adapt, as well as a certain blindness to the erroneousness of dividing the Real into a number of discrete domains. It is quite wrong to make a distinction between action on the psyche, the socius and the environment. Refusal to face up to the erosion of these three areas, as the media would have us do, verges on a strategic infantilization of opinion and a destructive neutralization of democracy. We need to 'kick the habit' of sedative discourse, particularly the 'fix' of television, in order to be able to apprehend the world through the interchangeable lenses or points of view of the three ecologies.

Chernobyl and AIDS have dramatically revealed to us the limits of humanity's techno-scientific power and the 'backlash' that 'nature' has in store for us. If the sciences and technology are to be directed towards more human ends, we evidently require collective forms of administration and control, rather than a blind faith in the technocrats of the State apparatuses; we cannot expect them to control progress and to avert risks in these domains, which are governed primarily by the principles of a profit economy. Of course, it would be absurd to want to return to the past in order to reconstruct former ways of living. After the data-processing and robotics revolutions, the rapid development of genetic engineering and the globalization of markets, neither human labour nor the natural habitat will ever be what they once were, even just a few decades ago. As Paul Virilio has suggested, the increased speed of transportation and communications and the interdependence of urban centres are equally irreversible.[35] While on the one hand we must make do with this situation, on the other we must acknowledge that it requires a reconstruction of the objectives and the methods of the whole of the social movement *under today's conditions*. To symbolize this problematic I need only refer to an experiment once conducted on television by Alain Bombard.[36] He produced two glass tanks, one filled with polluted water – of the sort that one might draw from the port of Marseille – containing a healthy, thriving, almost dancing octopus.[37] The other tank contained pure, unpolluted seawater. Bombard caught the octopus and immersed it in the 'normal' water; after a few seconds the animal curled up, sank to the bottom and died.

Now more than ever, nature cannot be separated from culture; in order to comprehend the interactions between ecosystems, the mechanosphere and the social and individual Universes of reference, we must learn to think 'transversally'. Just as monstrous and mutant algae invade the lagoon of Venice, so our television screens are populated, saturated, by 'degenerate' images and statements [*écnocés*].[38] In the field of social ecology, men like Donald Trump are permitted to proliferate freely, like another species of algae, taking over entire districts of New York and Atlantic City; he 'redevelops' by raising rents, thereby driving out tens of thousands of poor families, most of whom are condemned to homelessness, becoming the equivalent of the dead fish of environmental ecology.[39] Further proliferation is evident in the savage deterritorialization of the Third World, which simultaneously affects the cultural texture of its populations, its habitat, its immune systems, climate, etc. Child labour is another disaster of social ecology; it has actually become more prevalent now than it was in the nineteenth century! How do we regain control of such an auto-destructive and potentially catastrophic situation?[40] International organizations have only the most tenuous control of these phenomena which call for a fundamental change in attitudes. International solidarity, once the primary concern of trade unions and leftist parties, is now the sole responsibility of humanitarian organizations. Although Marx's own writings still have great value, Marxist discourse has lost its value. It is up to the protagonists of social liberation to remodel the theoretical references so as to illuminate a possible escape route out of contemporary history, which is more nightmarish than ever. It is not only species that are becoming extinct but also the words, phrases and gestures of human solidarity. A stifling cloak of silence has been thrown over the emancipatory struggles of women, and of the new proletariat: the unemployed, the 'marginalized', immigrants.

In mapping out the cartographic reference points of the three ecologies, it is important to dispense with pseudoscientific paradigms. This is not simply due to the complexity of the entities under consideration but more fundamentally to the fact that the three ecologies are governed by a *different logic* to that of ordinary communication between speakers and listeners which has nothing to do with the intelligibility of discursive sets, or the indeterminate interlocking of fields of signification. It is a logic of intensities, of auto-referential existential assemblages engaging in irreversible durations. It is the logic not only of human subjects constituted as totalized bodies, but also of psychoanalytic partial objects – what Winnicott calls transitional objects, institutional objects ('subject-groups'), faces and landscapes, etc.[41] While the logic of discursive sets endeavours to completely delimit its objects, the logic of intensities, or eco-logic, is concerned only with the movement and intensity of evolutive processes. Process, which I oppose here to system or to structure, strives to capture existence in the very act of its constitution, definition and deterritorialization.[42] This process of 'fixing-into-being' relates only to expressive subsets that have broken out of their totalizing frame and have begun to work on their own account, overcoming their referential sets and manifesting themselves as their own existential indices, processual lines of flight.

Ecological praxes strive to scout out the potential vectors of subjectification and singularization at each partial existential locus. They generally seek something that runs counter to the 'normal' order of things, a counter-repetition, an intensive given which invokes other intensities to form new existential configurations. These dissident vectors have become relatively detached from their denotative and significative functions and operate as decorporealized existential materials. However, as experiments in the suspension of meaning they are risky, as there is the possibility of a violent deterritorialization which would destroy the assemblage of subjectification (as was the case in Italy in the early 1980s, for example, with the implosion of the social movement). A more gentle deterritorialization, however, might enable the assemblages to evolve in a constructive, processual fashion. At the heart of all ecological praxes there is an a-signifying rupture, in which the catalysts of existential change are close at hand, but lack expressive support from the assemblage of enunciation; they therefore remain passive and are in danger of losing their consistency – here are to be found the roots of anxiety, guilt and, more generally, psychopathological repetitions [*réitérations*]. In the scenario of processual assemblages, the expressive a-signifying rupture summons forth a creative repetition that forges incorporeal objects, abstract machines and Universes of value that make their presence felt as though they had been always 'already there', although they are entirely dependent on the existential event that brings them into play.

Furthermore, these existential catalytic segments can also remain the bearers of denotation and signification. The ambiguity of a poetic text, for example, comes from the fact that it may both transmit a message or denote a referent while functioning at the same time through redundancies of expression and content. Proust skilfully analysed the function of these existential refrains as catalytic focal points of subjectification: Vinteuil's 'little phrase', for example, the ringing of the Martinville church bells or the flavour of the madeleine. What we must emphasize here is that the work of locating these existential refrains is not the sole province of literature and the arts – we find this eco-logic equally at work in everyday life, in social life at every level, and whenever the constitution of an existential Territory is in question. Let us add that these Territories may already have been deterritorialized to the extreme – they can embody themselves in a Heavenly Jerusalem, the problematic of good and evil, or any ethico-political commitment, etc. The only commonality that exists between these various existential features [*traits*] is their ability to maintain the production of singular existents or to resingularize serialized ensembles.

Throughout history and across the world existential cartographies founded on a conscious acceptance of certain 'existentializing' ruptures of meaning have sought refuge in art and religion. However, today the huge subjective void produced by the proliferating production of material and immaterial goods is becoming ever more absurd and increasingly irreparable and threatens the consistency of both individual and group existential Territories. While there no longer appears to be a cause-and-effect relationship between the growth in techno-scientific resources and the development of social and cultural progress, it seems clear that we are witnessing an irreversible erosion of the traditional mechanisms of social regulation. Faced with this situation, the most 'modernist' capitalist formations seem, in their own way, to be banking on a return to the past, however artificial, and on a reconstitution of ways of being that were familiar to our ancestors. We can see, for example, how certain hierarchical structures (having lost a significant part of their functional efficiency as a result, principally, of the computerization of information and organizational management) have become the object of an imaginary hypercathexis, at both upper and lower executive levels; in the example of Japan this hypercathexis occasionally verges on religious devotion.[43] Similarly we are witnessing a reinforcement of segregationist attitudes vis-à-vis immigrants, women, the young and the elderly. Such a rise in what we might call a subjective conservatism is not solely attributable to an intensification of social repression; it stems equally from a kind of existential contraction [*crispation*] involving all of the actors in the socius. Post-industrial capitalism, which I prefer to describe as *Integrated World Capitalism* (IWC), tends increasingly to decentre its sites of power, moving away from structures producing goods and services towards structures producing signs, syntax and – in particular, through the control which it exercises over the media, advertising, opinion polls, etc. – subjectivity.

This evolution ought to make us reflect upon the ways in which earlier forms of capitalism operated, given that they too were not exempt from this same tendency towards the capitalization of subjective power, both at the level of the capitalist élites as well as among the proletariat. However, the true importance of this propensity within capitalism was never fully demonstrated, with the result that it was not properly appreciated by theoreticians of the workers' movement.

I would propose grouping together four main semiotic regimes, the mechanisms [*instruments*] on which IWC is founded:

(1) *Economic semiotics* (monetary, financial, accounting and decision-making mechanisms);

(2) *Juridical semiotics* (title deeds, legislation and regulations of all kinds);

(3) *Techno-scientific semiotics* (plans, diagrams, programmes, studies, research, etc.);

(4) *Semiotics of subjectification*, of which some coincide with those already mentioned, but to which we should add many others, such as those relating to architecture, town planning, public facilities, etc.

We must acknowledge that models which claim to found a causal hierarchy between these semiotic regimes are well on their way to completely losing touch with reality. For example, it becomes increasingly difficult to maintain that economic semiotics and semiotics that work together towards the production of material goods occupy an infrastructural position in relation to juridical and ideological semiotics, as was postulated by Marxism. At present, IWC is all of a piece: productive–economic–subjective. And, to return to the old scholastic categories, one might say that it follows at the same time from material, formal, efficient and final causes.[44]

One of the key analytic problems confronted by social and mental ecology is the introjection of repressive power by the oppressed.[45] The major difficulty here is the fact that the unions and the parties, which struggle, in principle, to defend the interests of the workers and the oppressed, reproduce in themselves the same pathogenic models that stifle all freedom of expression and innovation in their own ranks. Perhaps it will still be necessary for a lapse of time to ensue before the workers' movement recognizes that the economic-ecological vectors of circulation, distribution, communication, supervision, and so on, are strictly situated on the same plane, from the point of view of the creation of surplus value, as labour that is directly incorporated into the production of material goods.[46] In this regard, a dogmatic ignorance has been maintained by a number of theoreticians, which only serves to reinforce a workerism and a corporatism that have profoundly distorted and handicapped anticapitalist movements of emancipation over the last few decades.

It is to be hoped that the development of the three types of ecological praxis outlined here will lead to a reframing and a recomposition of the goals of the emancipatory struggles. And let us hope that, in the context of the new 'deal' of the relation between capital and human activity, ecologists, feminists, antiracists, etc. will make it an immediate major objective to target the modes of production of subjectivity, that is, of knowledge, culture, sensibility and sociability that come under an incorporeal value system at the root of the new productive assemblages.

Social ecology will have to work towards rebuilding human relations at every level of the socius. It should never lose sight of the fact that capitalist power has become delocalized and deterritorilized, both in extension, by extending its influence over the whole social, economic and cultural life of the planet, and in 'intension', by infiltrating the most unconscious subjective strata. In doing this it is no longer possible to claim to be opposed to capitalist power only from the outside, through trade unions and traditional politics. It is equally imperative to confront capitalism's effects in the domain of mental ecology in everyday life: individual, domestic, material, neighbourly, creative or one's personal ethics. Rather than looking for a stupefying and infantalizing consensus, it will be a question in the future of cultivating a *dissensus* and the singular production of existence. A capitalistic subjectivity is engendered through operators of all types and sizes, and is manufactured to protect existence from any intrusion of events that might disturb or disrupt public opinion. It demands that all singularity must be either evaded or crushed in specialist apparatuses and frames of reference. Therefore, it endeavours to manage the worlds of childhood, love, art, as well as everything associated with anxiety, madness, pain, death, or a feeling of being lost in the Cosmos

. . . IWC forms massive subjective aggregates from the most personal – one could even say infra-personal – existential givens, which it hooks up to ideas of race, nation, the professional workforce, competitive sports, a dominating masculinity [*virilité*], mass-media celebrity . . . Capitalistic subjectivity seeks to gain power by controlling and neutralizing the maximum number of existential refrains. It is intoxicated with and anaesthetized by a collective feeling of pseudo-eternity.[47]

It seems to me that the new ecological practices will have to articulate themselves on these many tangled and heterogeneous fronts, their objective being to processually activate isolated and repressed singularities that are just turning in circles. (For example, a school class in which are applied the principles of the Freinet School aims to singularize the overall functioning through cooperative systems, assessment meetings, a newspaper, the pupils' freedom to organize their own work individually or in groups, etc.)[48]

From this same perspective we will have to consider symptoms and incidents outside the norm as indices of a potential labour of subjectification. It seems to me essential to organize new micropolitical and microsocial practices, new solidarities, a new gentleness, together with new aesthetic and new analytic practices regarding the formation of the unconscious. It appears to me that this is the only possible way to get social and political practices back on their feet, working for humanity and not simply for a permanent reequilibration of the capitalist semiotic Universe. One might object that large-scale struggles are not necessarily in sync with ecological praxis and the micropolitics of desire, but that's the point: it is important not to homogenize various levels of practice or to make connections between them under some transcendental supervision, but instead to engage them in processes of *heterogenesis*.[49] Feminists will never take a becoming-woman far enough, and there is no reason to demand that immigrants should renounce their nationalitarian belonging or the cultural traits that cling to their very being.[50] Particular cultures should be left to deploy themselves in inventing other contracts of citizenship. Ways should be found to enable the singular, the exceptional, the rare, to coexist with a State structure that is the least burdensome possible.

Unlike Hegelian and Marxist dialectics, eco-logic no longer imposes a 'resolution' of opposites. In the domain of social ecology there will be times of struggle in which everyone will feel impelled to decide on common objectives and to act 'like little soldiers', by which I mean like good activists. But there will simultaneously be periods in which individual and collective subjectivities will 'pull out' without a thought for collective aims, and in which creative expression as such will take precedence. This new ecosophical logic – and I want to emphasize this point – resembles the manner in which an artist may be led to alter his work after the intrusion of some accidental detail, an event-incident that suddenly makes his initial project bifurcate, making it drift [*dériver*] far from its previous path, however certain it had once appeared to be.[51] There is a proverb 'the exception proves the rule', but the exception can just as easily deflect the rule, or even re-create it.

Environmental ecology, as it exists today, has barely begun to prefigure the generalized ecology that I advocate here, the aim of which will be to radically decentre social struggles and ways of coming to one's own psyche. Current ecological movements certainly have merit, but in truth I think that the overall ecosophical question is too important to be left to some of its usual archaizers and folklorists, who sometimes deliberately refuse any large-scale political involvement. Ecology must stop being associated with the image of a small nature-loving minority or with qualified specialists. Ecology in my sense questions the whole of subjectivity and capitalistic power formations, whose sweeping progress cannot be guaranteed to continue as it has for the past decade.

The present ongoing crisis, both financial and economic, could not only lead to important upheavals of the social status-quo and the mass-media imaginary that underlies it, but certain themes promoted by neo-liberalists – such as flexible labour, deregulation, etc. – could perfectly well backfire on them.

I stress once again, the choice is no longer simply between blind fixation to old State-bureaucratic supervision and generalized welfare on the one hand, and a despairing and cynical surrender to 'yuppie' ideology on the other. All the indications suggest that the productivity gains engendered by current technological revolutions will inscribe themselves on a curve of logarithmic growth. Henceforth it is a question of knowing whether the new ecological operators and the new ecosophical assemblages of enunciation will succeed in channelling these gains in less absurd, less dead-ended directions than those of Integrated World Capitalism.

The principle common to the three ecologies is this: each of the existential Territories with which they confront us is not given as an in-itself [*en-soi*], closed in on itself, but instead as a for-itself [*pour-soi*] that is precarious, finite, finitized, singular, singularized, capable of bifurcating into stratified and deathly repetitions or of opening up processually from a praxis that enables it to be made 'habitable' by a human project. It is this praxic opening-out which constitutes the essence of 'eco'-art.[52] It subsumes all existing ways of domesticating existential Territories and is concerned with intimate modes of being, the body, the environment or large contextual ensembles relating to ethnic groups, the nation, or even the general rights of humanity. Having said this, it is not a question of establishing universal rules as a guide to this praxis, but on the contrary of setting forth the principle antinomies between the ecosophical levels, or, if you prefer, between the three ecological visions, the three discriminating lenses under discussion here.

The principle specific to mental ecology is that its approach to existential Territories derives from a pre-objectal and pre-personal logic of the sort that Freud has described as being a 'primary process'.[53] One could call this the logic of the 'included middle', in which black and white are indistinct, where the beautiful coexists with the ugly, the inside with the outside, the 'good' object with the 'bad'. . .[54] In the particular case of the ecology of the phantasm, each attempt to locate it cartographically requires the drafting of an expressive framework that is both singular and, more precisely, singularized.[55] Gregory Bateson has clearly shown that what he calls the 'ecology of ideas' cannot be contained within the domain of the psychology of the individual, but organizes itself into systems or 'minds', the boundaries of which no longer coincide with the participant individuals.[56] But I part company with Bateson when he treats action and enunciation as mere parts of an ecological subsystem called 'context'.[57] I myself consider that existential taking on of context is always brought about by a praxis which is established in the rupture of the systemic 'pretext'. There is no overall hierarchy for locating and localizing the components of enunciation at a given level. They are composed of heterogeneous elements that take on a mutual consistency and persistence as they cross the thresholds that constitute one world at the expense of another. The operators of this crystallization are fragments of a-signifying chains of the type that Schlegel likens to works of art. ('A fragment like a miniature work of art must be totally detached from the surrounding world and closed on itself like a hedgehog'.)[58]

The question of mental ecology may emerge anywhere, at any moment, beyond fully constituted ensembles on the order of the individual and the collective. In order to arrest these fragments that act as catalysts in existential bifurcations, Freud invented the rituals of the session – free association, interpretation – according to the psychoanalytical myths of reference. Today, certain post-systemic tendencies in family therapy have set about creating different scenes and references. That's all well and good, but these conceptual scaffoldings still do not take into account the production of 'primary' subjectivity, because they are deployed on a truly industrial scale, particularly by the media and public institutions. All existing theoretical bodies of this type share the shortcoming of being closed to the possibility of creative proliferation. Whether they be myths or theories with scientific pretensions, the relevance of such models to mental ecology must be decided by the following criteria:

(1) their capacity to recognize discursive chains at the point when they break with meaning;

(2) the use they make of concepts that allow for a theoretical and practical auto-constructability.

Freudianism meets the first condition reasonably well, but not the second. On the other hand, post-systemism is more likely to meet the second condition while wholly underestimating the first, since, in the socio-political field, 'alternative' milieus generally misunderstand the whole range of problematics relevant to mental ecology.

For our part, we advocate a rethinking of the various attempts at 'psychiatric' modelling, in much the same way as one would approach the practices of religious sects, the 'family novels' of neurotics or the deliriums of psychotics.[59] It will be less a question of taking stock of these practices in terms of their scientific veracity than according to their aesthetico-existential effectiveness. What do we find? What existential scenes establish themselves there? The crucial objective is to grasp the a-signifying points of rupture – the rupture of denotation, connotation and signification – from which a certain number of semiotic chains are put to work in the service of an existential autoreferential effect. The repetitive symptom, the prayer, the ritual of the 'session', the order-word, the emblem, the refrain, the facialitary crystallization of the celebrity . . . initiates the production of a partial subjectivity.[60] We can say that they are the beginnings of a *protosubjectivity*. The Freudians had already detected the existence of vectors of subjectification that elude the mastery of the Self; partial subjectivity, complexual,[61] taking shape around objects in the rupture of meaning, such as the maternal breast, faeces, the genitals . . .[62] But these objects, the generators of a breakaway or 'dissident' subjectivity, were conceived by Freudians as residing essentially adjacent to the instinctual urges and to a corporealized imaginary. Other institutional objects, be they architectural, economic or Cosmic, have an equal right to contribute to the functioning of existential production.

I repeat: the essential thing here is the break-bifurcation, which it is impossible to represent as such, but which nevertheless exudes a phantasmatic of origins (the Freudian primal scene, initiation ceremonies, conjuration, the 'armed gaze' of the systematician of family therapy, etc.). Pure creative auto-reference is impossible in the apprehension of ordinary existence. Attempts to represent it can only succeed in masking it, travestying it, disfiguring it, making it pass through mythic and narrative myths of reference – what I call metamodelization.[63] Corollary: These focal points of creative subjectification in their nascent state can only be accessed by the detour of a phantasmatic economy that is deployed in a random form. In short, no one is exempt from playing the game of the ecology of the imaginary!

In order to have an impact on individual and collective life, mental ecology does not presuppose the importing of concepts and practices from a specialized 'psychiatric' domain. It demands instead that we face up to the logic of desiring ambivalence wherever it emerges – in culture, everyday life, work, sport, etc. – in order to reevaluate the purpose of work and of human activities according to different criteria than those of profit and yield. The imperatives of mental ecology call for an appropriate mobilization of individuals and social segments as a whole. It raises the question of the place we give to phantasms of aggression, murder, rape and racism in the world of childhood and of a regressive adulthood. Rather than tirelessly implementing procedures of censorship and contention in the name of great moral principles we should learn how to promote a true ecology of the phantasm, one that works through the transference, translation and redeployment of their matters of expression.[64] It is, of course, legitimate to repress the 'acting out' of certain fantasies! But initially it is necessary for even negative and destructive phantasmagorias to acquire modes of expression – as in the treatment of psychosis – that allow them to be 'abreacted' in order to reanchor existential Territories that are drifting away.[65] This sort of 'transversalization' of violence does not presuppose the need to deal with the existence of an intrapsychic death drive that constantly lies in wait, ready to ravage everything in its path as soon as the Territories of the Self lose their consistency and vigilance. Violence and negativity are the products of complex subjective assemblages; they are not intrinsically inscribed in the essence of the human species, but are constructed and maintained by multiple assemblages of enunciation. Sade and Celine both endeavoured, with more or less success, to turn their negative fantasies into quasi-baroque ones, and because of this they may be considered as key authors for a mental ecology. Any persistently intolerant and uninventive society that fails to 'imaginarize' the various manifestations of violence risks seeing this violence crystallized in the Real.

We see it today, for example, in the intensive commercial exploitation of scatological comic books aimed at children.[66] But in many ways a lot more disturbing is the fascinating and repulsive species of the one-eyed man, who knows better than anyone how to force his implicitly racist and Nazi discourse onto the French media and into the political arena.[67] We should not ignore the fact that the power of this sort of character resides in his ability to interpret an entire montage of drives, which in fact haunt *all of the socius*.

I am not so naive and utopian as to maintain that there exists a reliable, analytic methodology that would be able to fundamentally eradicate all of the fantasies leading to the objectification of women, immigrants, the insane, etc., or that might allow us to have done with prisons and psychiatric institutions, etc.[68] However it does seem to me that a generalization of the experiences of institutional analysis (in hospitals, schools, the urban environment) might profoundly modify the conditions of this problem [*les données de ce problème*]. There will have to be a massive reconstruction of social mechanisms [*rouages*] if we are to confront the damage caused by IWC. It will not come about through centralized reform, through laws, decrees and bureaucratic programmes, but rather through the promotion of innovatory practices, the expansion of alternative experiences centred around a respect for singularity, and through the continuous production of an autonomizing subjectivity that can articulate itself appropriately in relation to the rest of society. Creating a space for violent fantasies – brutal deterritorializations of the psyche and of the socius – won't lead to miraculous sublimation, but only to redeployed assemblages that will overflow the body, the Self and the individual in all directions. Ordinary approaches to education and socialization won't weaken the grip of a punitive superego or deathly guilt complex. The great religions, apart from Islam, have an increasingly insignificant hold over the psyche, while almost everywhere else in the world, we are seeing a kind of return to totemism and animism. Troubled human communities tend to become introspective and abandon the task of governing or managing society to the professional politicians, while trade unions are left behind by the mutations of a society that is everywhere in latent or manifest crisis.[69]

The principle specific to social ecology concerns the development of affective and pragmatic cathexis [*investissement*] in human groups of differing sizes.[70] This 'groupEros' doesn't present itself as an abstract quantity but corresponds to a specifically qualitative reorganization [*reconversion*] of primary subjectivity as it relates to mental ecology.[71] Two options present themselves: a personological triangulation – I–YOU–S/HE, Father–Mother–Child – or in terms of autoreferential *subject-groups*, which open broadly onto the socius and the Cosmos. In the first instance, the Self and the other are constructed through a set of stock identifications and imitations, which result in primary groups that are refolded on the father, the boss, or the mass-media celebrity – this is the psychology of the pliable masses upon which the media practices.[72] In the second instance, identificatory systems are replaced by traits of diagrammatic efficiency.[73] An at least partial escape here from the semiologies of iconic modelling in favour of processual semiotics (which I will resist calling symbolic to avoid falling into the bad habits of the structuralists). A diagrammatic trait, as opposed to an icon, is characterized by the degree of its deterritorialization, its capacity to escape from itself in order to constitute discursive chains directly in touch with the referent. There is a distinction, for example, between a piano pupil's identificatory imitation of his teacher and the transference of a style likely to bifurcate in a singular direction. There is also a more general distinction to be made between imaginary crowd aggregates and collective assemblages of enunciation, which conjoin pre-personal traits with social systems or their machinic components (here I am opposing living autopoietic machines to mechanisms of empty repetition).[74]

Having said all this, the oppositions between these two modalities of group formation are not really so clear cut: a crowd might be inhabited by opinion-leading groups and subject-groups may revert to amorphous and alienating states of being. Capitalist societies – and here I include not only Japan and the Western powers, but also the so-called truly socialist countries and the new industrial powers of the Third World – produce, for their own ends, three types of subjectivity. Firstly, a serial subjectivity corresponding to the salaried classes, secondly, to the huge mass of the 'uninsured' [*nongarantis*] and, finally, an elitist subjectivity corresponding to the executive sectors. The accelerating mass-mediatization of global societies tends, therefore, to create an increasing divergence between these different population categories.[75] For their part, the élites possess material wealth, sufficient cultural capital, a minimal level of reading and writing, and a sense of competence and legitimate decision-making power. In contrast, the subjugated classes, on the whole, are abandoned to the status quo – life for them is hopeless and meaningless. An essential programmatic point for social ecology will be to encourage capitalist societies to make the transition from the mass-media era to a *post-media age*, in which the media will be reappropriated by a multitude of subject-groups capable of directing its resingularization. Despite the seeming impossibility of such an eventuality, the currently unparalleled level of media-related alienation is in no way an inherent necessity. It seems to me that media fatalism equates to a misunderstanding of a number of factors:

(1) sudden mass consciousness-raising, which always remains possible;

(2) the progressive collapse of Stalinism in all its incarnations, which leaves room for other transformative assemblages of social struggle;

(3) the technological evolution of the media and its possible use for non-capitalist goals, in particular through a reduction in costs and through miniaturization;

(4) the reconstitution of labour processes on the rubble of early twentieth-century systems of industrial production, based upon the increased production – as much on an individual basis as on a collective one – of a 'creationist' subjectivity (achieved through continuous training, skill transfer and the 're-tooling' [*ressourcement*] of the labour force, etc.).[76]

In early industrial society, it was the subjectivity of the working classes that was eroded [*laminer*] and serialized. Today, the international division of labour has been exported to the Third World where production-line methods now prevail. In this era of the information revolution, biotechnological expansion, the accelerated invention of new materials and ever more precise 'machinization' of time, new modalities of subjectification are continually emerging.[77] On the one hand, a greater demand will be placed on intelligence and initiative, whereas on the other hand, more care will be taken over the coding and control of the domestic life of married couples and nuclear families. In short, by reterritorializing the family on a large scale (through the media, the welfare system, etc.), an attempt will be made to achieve the maximum middle-classification [*embourgeoiser*] of working-class subjectivity.

The effects of these processes of reindividualization and 'familialization' won't all be the same. They will differ according to whether they affect a collective subjectivity devastated by the industrial era of the nineteenth and early twentieth century or areas where certain archaic features of the pre-capitalist era have been inherited and maintained. In this context, the examples of Japan and Italy seem significant because both countries have succeeded in grafting high-tech industries onto a collective subjectivity, while retaining ties with a sometimes very distant past (Shinto–Buddhism in the case of Japan, patriarchalism in the case of Italy). In both of these countries, post-industrialization has been achieved with comparatively little violence, whereas in France for example, for a long time whole regions withdrew from the active economic life of the country.

In a number of Third World countries we are also witnessing the superimposition of a post-industrial subjectivity onto a medieval subjectivity, as evidenced by submission to the clan, the total alienation of women and children, etc. Although currently confined primarily to the Pacific Rim, these New Industrial Powers may well begin to flourish along the shores of the Mediterranean and Atlantic coasts of Africa. If they do, we may well see entire regions of Europe subject to severe tensions; they will radically challenge not only Europe's financial base but the membership status of its countries in the Great White Power club.

As the above indicates, ecological problematics can become somewhat confused. Left to itself, the propagation of social and mental neo-archaisms could be for the best, or for the worst – a formidably difficult question to resolve – especially when we recall that the fascism of the Ayatollahs was installed firmly on the basis of a profoundly popular revolution in Iran. The recent uprisings of young people in Algeria have fostered a double symbiosis between Western ways of living and various forms of fundamentalism. Spontaneous social ecology works towards the constitution of existential Territories that replace, more or less, the former religious and ritualized griddings of the socius. It seems evident that, unless a politically coherent stance is taken by collective praxes, social ecology will ultimately always be dominated by reactionary nationalist enterprises hostile to any innovation, oppressing women, children and the marginalized. I am not proposing a ready-made model of society here, but simply the acceptance of a complete range of ecosophical components so as to institute, in particular, new systems of valorization.

I have already stressed that it is less and less legitimate that only a profit-based market should regulate financial and prestige-based rewards for human social activities, for there is a range of other value systems that ought to be considered, including social and aesthetic 'profitability' and the values of desire. Until now, these non-capitalist domains of value have only been regulated by the State; hence, for example, the esteem in which national heritage is held. We must stress that new social associations – such as institutions recognized for their social utility – should broaden the financing of a more flexible non-private, non-public Third Sector, which will be forced to expand continuously for as long as human labour gives way to machinization. Beyond recognizing a universal basic income – as a *right* rather than as some kind of 'New Deal' – the question becomes one of how to encourage the organization of individual and collective ventures, and how to direct them towards an ecology of resingularization. The search for an existential Territory or homeland doesn't necessarily involve searching for one's country of birth or a distant country of origin, although too often, nationalitarian movements (like the Irish or the Basques) have turned in on themselves due to exterior antagonisms, leaving aside other molecular revolutions relating to women's liberation, environmental ecology, etc. All sorts of deterritorialized 'nationalities' are conceivable, such as music and poetry. What condemns the capitalist value system is that it is characterized by general equivalence, which flattens out all other forms of value, alienating them in its hegemony. On this basis we must if not oppose, at least superimpose instruments of valorization founded on existential productions that cannot be determined simply in terms of abstract labour-time or by an expected capitalist profit. The information and telematic revolutions are supporting new 'stock exchanges' of value and new collective debate, providing opportunities for the most individual, most singular and most dissensual enterprises. The notion of collective interest ought to be expanded to include companies that, in the short term, don't profit anyone, but in the long term are the conduits of a processual enrichment for the whole of humanity. It is the whole future of fundamental research and artistic production that is in question here.

It must also be stressed that this promotion of existential values and the values of desire will not present itself as a fully-fledged global alternative. It will result from widespread shifts in current value systems and from the appearance of new poles of valorization. In this respect it is significant that, over the last few years, the most spectacular social changes have resulted from precisely these kinds of long-term shifts; on a political level in the Philippines or Chile, for example, or on a nationalitary level in the USSR.[78] In these countries, thousands of value-system revolutions are progressively percolating their way up through society and it is up to the new ecological components to polarize them and to affirm their importance within the political and social relations of force.

There is a principle specific to environmental ecology: it states that anything is possible – the worst disasters or the most flexible evolutions [*évolutions en souplesse*].[79] Natural equilibriums will be increasingly reliant upon human intervention, and a time will come when vast programmes will need to be set up in order to regulate the relationship between oxygen, ozone and carbon dioxide in the Earth's atmosphere. We might just as well rename environmental ecology *machinic ecology*, because Cosmic and human praxis has only ever been a question of machines, even, dare I say it, of war machines.[80] From time immemorial 'nature' has been at war with life! The pursuit of mastery over the mechanosphere will have to begin immediately if the acceleration of techno-scientific progress and the pressure of huge population increases are to be dealt with.

In the future much more than the simple defence of nature will be required; we will have to launch an initiative if we are to repair the Amazonian 'lung', for example, or bring vegetation back to the Sahara. The creation of new living species – animal and vegetable – looms inevitably on the horizon, and the adoption of an ecosophical ethics adapted to this terrifying and fascinating situation is equally as urgent as the invention of a politics focussed on the destiny of humanity.

As new stories of the permanent re-creation of the world replace the narrative of biblical genesis, we can do no better than cite Walter Benjamin, condemning the reductionism that accompanies the primacy of information:

When information supplants the old form, storytelling, and when it itself gives way to sensation, this double process reflects an imaginary degradation of experience. Each of these forms is in its own way an offshoot of storytelling. Storytelling . . . does not aim to convey the pure essence of a thing, like information or a report. It sinks the thing into the life of the storyteller, in order to bring it out of him again. Thus traces of the storyteller cling to the story the way the handprints of the potter cling to the clay vessel.[81]

To bring into being other worlds beyond those of purely abstract information; to engender Universes of reference and existential Territories where singularity and finitude are taken into consideration by the multivalent logic of mental ecologies and by the group Eros principle of social ecology; to dare to confront the vertiginous Cosmos so as to make it inhabitable – these are the tangled paths of the tri-ecological vision.

A new ecosophy, at once applied and theoretical, ethico-political and aesthetic, would have to move away from the old forms of political, religious and associative commitment . . . Rather than being a discipline of refolding on interiority, or a simple renewal of earlier forms of 'militancy', it will be a multifaceted movement, deploying agencies [*instances*] and dispositives that will simultaneously analyse and produce subjectivity. A collective and individual subjectivity that completely exceeds the limits of individualization, stagnation, identificatory closure, and will instead open itself up on all sides to the socius, but also to the machinic Phylum, to techno-scientific Universes of reference, to aesthetic worlds, as well as to a new 'pre-personal' understanding of time, of the body, of sexuality. A subjectivity of resingularization that can meet head-on the encounter with the finitude of desire, pain and death. However, rumour would have it that none of this is self-evident! All sorts of neuroleptic cloaks [*chapes*] enshroud this subjectivity, concealing it from any intrusive singularity.[82] Do we have to invoke History yet again? There is at least a risk that there will be no more human history unless humanity undertakes a radical reconsideration of itself. We must ward off, by every means possible, the entropic rise of a dominant subjectivity. Rather than remaining subject, in perpetuity, to the seductive efficiency of economic competition, we must reappropriate Universes of value, so that processes of singularization can rediscover their consistency. We need new social and aesthetic practices, new practices of the Self in relation to the other, to the foreign, the strange – a whole programme that seems far removed from current concerns. And yet, ultimately, we will only escape from the major crises of our era through the articulation of:

– a nascent subjectivity;

– a constantly mutating socius;

– an environment in the process of being reinvented.

In conclusion, it should be understood that the three ecologies originate from a common ethico-aesthetic discipline, and are also distinct from the point of view of the practices that characterize them. Their different styles are produced by what I call *heterogenesis*, in other words, processes of continuous resingularization. Individuals must become both more united and increasingly different. The same is true for the resingularization of schools, town councils, urban planning, etc.

By means of these transversal tools [*clefs*], subjectivity is able to install itself simultaneously in the realms of the environment, in the major social and institutional assemblages, and symmetrically in the landscapes and fantasies of the most intimate spheres of the individual. The reconquest of a degree of creative autonomy in one particular domain encourages conquests in other domains – the catalyst for a gradual reforging and renewal of humanity's confidence in itself starting at the most minuscule level. Hence this essay, which sets out, in its own way, to counter the pervasive atmosphere of dullness and passivity.[83]

The Life and Work of Félix Guattari: From Transversality to Ecosophy

Gary Genosko

Transversality is a vitally important concept in Félix Guattari's theoretical and political vocabulary. His essay 'Transversalité', dating from 1964, has been available in French since 1972, and an English translation – recognized as flawed but serviceable in its literalness, especially when considered in relation to many of the other translations undertaken by Rosemary Sheed in the out-of-print *Molecular Revolution* (Guattari, 1984) – has not attracted much direct commentary. Since the concept appears throughout Guattari's published work, and the seminal concomitant distinction between subject groups and subjugated groups has been revisited by Guattari in his collaborations with Gilles Deleuze most notably in *Anti-Oedipus* (Deleuze and Guattari, 1984), as well as in his own writings and been rigorously applied to a literary text by Brian Massumi (1988), following the model of Deleuze's application of it in his essay 'The Literary Machine' from a later edition of *Proust and Signs* (Deleuze, 1972), it may have escaped comment because of its obviousness; or, perhaps, it has been overshadowed by or simply conflated with schizoanalysis. Whatever the case may be, everyone in the field seems to know what it means; still, much is presupposed about the concept's infancy. Recent work on Guattari has traced the concept's origins (Bosteels, 1998: 145–74) to certain passages in Louis Althusser and Jean-Paul Sartre, although Guattari was the first to fully develop and apply it.

Nowhere is it explained what Guattari meant by the relation between the modification of the objects incorporated (technically introjected) by the superego, which leads to nothing less than a dehabituation of the superego to its police operations, and the function of transversality, a relation he dwells on at length while exploring its practical and political implications. The superego is, after all, a tough nut to crack since, according to Freud, it is primarily coloured by one's parents (especially one's father) but is also open to later influences such as the media, as well as a variety of archaic influences (some phylogenetic inheritances), not to mention long-abandoned objects, which places it in the topography farther from consciousness than the ego. There are a few concentrated bursts about transversality in interviews, and Guattari does, here and there in his published work, reflect on several of his somewhat awkward and orthodox early formulations, but nothing more sustained. Indeed, a mere two years after the 'Transversalité' essay, Guattari remarked in passing that 'in different places and under different circumstances, I advanced different things: for example, I spoke of the "objects introjected by the superego" . . .' (1972: 151). His repeated use of the word 'different' underlines how much his attitude had changed in such a short time (from 1964 to 1966, to be precise), and it makes all the difference to read this repetition as an affirmation of change as opposed to the symptom of a fixation.

Not only, then, is an explication of the concept long overdue, but such an explication needs to be placed in the context of Guattari's subsequent deployments of it; none of which are as concentrated as his original paper, and many of which diverge in an interesting manner from his early considerations. One can imagine that for those readers unfamiliar with the concept's development and the slow moulting of its psychoanalytic shell, its adjectival deployments may seem to simply multiply, while at the same time the substance of the concept becomes less and less stable, acquiring a second-order existence of formal emptiness (empty of history, reality and contingency), while remaining rich in meaning, opening itself to postmodern appropriations without practical consequences for any person or institution, which would not be in the spirit of Guattari's thought.

The concept's mutation over time is a consequence of the array of new ideas with which it intersects in Guattari's later writings. It must not be forgotten that the concept of transversality had for Guattari practical tasks to perform in specific institutional settings. Transversality was not a philosophical but a political concept, and one never loses the impression, despite the heavy Freudianism of the early Guattari, that the idea was to use it imaginatively in order to change, perhaps not the entire world, but institutions as we know them, beginning with analytic method.

The excavation and explication of the concept of transversality is my choice means by which to present an introduction to the life and work of Guattari. It is a thread, to use one of Freud's favourite metaphors, that may be pulled in order to unravel a life because it is central and continuous. It is, however, not without its knots, tangles, colour changes, weak points and intersections; in the end, these only make it more interesting.

The key signposts along the way are, firstly, transference and the concept's psychoanalytic scaffolding; secondly, the coefficients of transversality; thirdly, the debt of his theory of groups to Jean-Paul Sartre's dialectical sociology. Having reached this point, I will then fourthly show how Guattari used the concept in his analytic practice at La Borde; fifthly, I compare and contrast Guattari's early with his later uses of transversality through a reflection on the relevance of transversality for ecosophy.

From Transference to Transversality

Guattari developed the concept of transversality through his interest in finding a kind of therapy adequate to an institutional context; in other words, what happens to classical psychotherapeutic technique focussed on the cure of an individual on a couch when the environment changes to a psychiatric hospital? What becomes of both technique and its theoretical aims in the hospital? Guattari's institutional work at the Clinique de La Borde called into question the analytic relation of analyst–analysand, the so-called face-to-face, dual relation, for the sake of the analysis of groups in a clinical setting. The institution, Guattari argued, was not simply a 'backdrop' against which classical dual analyses might be undertaken, regardless of their Freudian or Lacanian lineage. The analyst had to come to terms with the effects of the setting on how s/he would normally proceed. Indeed, the analyst was called upon to translate and reevaluate technical and conceptual notions in relation to what Guattari called the 'institutional object'.

The straight gate to the critique of psychoanalysis was through the transference relation because it is the cornerstone of psychoanalytic method; the transference is a libidinal tie between the analysand and analyst, the stage upon which everything that is pathological in the patient may be rehearsed, as it were. It is an aid to the analysis (the analyst must take advantage of the love the analysand feels for him or her for this love is an important manifestation of the transference and must be dealt with, ultimately, dismantled piece by piece), but also a force of resistance. As mischievous and seductive as the transference can be, it is the *sine qua non* of a successful treatment. Once it is dislodged and the dual analysis sidestepped, the full effects of the 'institutional object' may be appreciated. Guattari's critical appreciation of transference took place through an analysis of the subjectivity of groups and involved the understanding of how places of treatment such as psychiatric hospitals may themselves actually prevent treatment, having been 'radically diverted from their manifest social finality' (Guattari, 1972: 90–1) to such an extent that they reinforce and exaggerate the existing problems of the patients in their care. The concept of transversality is fundamental to the critique of the psychiatric hospital and therapeutic method. It is fair to say that it represents Guattari's first major theoretical contribution; put simply, transversality was Guattari's answer to the transference when it was critically reevaluated in the context of the treatment of groups of patients in a hospital setting.

With this outline in mind, we can continue. In his training analysis with Jacques Lacan – which lasted some seven years from 1962 to

1969 – and critical reading of the texts of Freud on the transference relation, Guattari had already learned to despise the transference because it was, as he wrote: 'fixed, insolubly mechanical . . . obligatory, predetermined, "territorialized" on a role, a given stereotype, making it worse than a resistance to analysis; it's a kind of internalization of bourgeois repression by the repetitive, archaic and artificial reappearance of caste phenomena with their procession of fascinating and reactionary group phantasms' (1972: 79). The transference is an artifact of the analysis, and hence artificial; it is also, Guattari strongly implied, an effect contributing to guruism in psychoanalysis. While Freud's own reflections on transference over the course of his remarks on technique shifted markedly from his view of it as a therapeutic alliance to a form of resistance, Guattari goes far beyond this creeping scepticism. The dual analysis was, in Guattari's experience, subject to various sorts of mystification because of the perverse deflection of the transference into a cult of an absolute master who, famously, 'founded, alone', and rebaptized psychoanalysis in the waters of structuralism, but whose retreats into aestheticism not only spoke volumes of his contempt for the lives of his patients, but cultivated a legion of sycophantic followers and fascistic lieutenants; this was, essentially, Guattari's objection to Lacan's Ecole freudienne.[1]

This may have been Guattari's political position on the 'school', but his theoretical suspicions were also much in evidence. In an essay originally published in 1964, 'The Transference', Guattari foils the expectations of readers of *Anti-Oedipus* with a bone to pick about triangulation, when he wrote: '. . . in the transference there is virtually never any actual dual relation . . . At the moment we envisage this relation [of mother and child] in a real situation we recognize that it is, at the very least, triangular in character. In other words, there is always in a real situation a mediating object that acts as an ambiguous support or medium' (Guattari, 1996b: 63). Those readers who have internalized the lessons of *Anti-Oedipus*, especially the critique of Oedipal triangulation, need to keep in mind that Guattari's early work sometimes contained accommodations of triangularity.[2] So, let's not get ahead of ourselves. What exactly did he mean by this? The 'real situation' is institutional life and the 'mediating object' is the group taken in context. Guattari is borrowing not so much from his teacher Lacan, but from D. W. Winnicott. And the triangle in question is not the famous Mummy–Daddy–Me but, instead, a third factor that is not strictly speaking a thing at all but a space, that is, the institutional object.

What is the institutional object, as it were, of transference in its new environment? Hospital/clinic-based psychotherapy requires a critique of the institution. One of the means by which this is accomplished will be through transversality because this foregrounds the institutional context, its constraints, organization, practices, etc., all those things and relations which normally exist in the background; in short, the group is how one gets at the institution. The idea of an institutional object captured, for Guattari, the massive conjugation of all of the effects on individuals and bureaucracies (patients, analysts, administrators), on theoretical concepts and analytic practices and goals, of the hospital setting. His reference to the 'mediating object' suggests, a matter he mentioned in passing in a footnote (Guattari, 1972: 82n.7), that he was modelling his institutional object on Winnicott's transitional object but using it in a more general way.

Like Winnicott's transitional object, Guattari's institutional object is not really a thing as such; indeed, things as such are not transitional. Rather, transitional phenomena occur in an 'intermediate area of experience' and a 'potential space' posited by Winnicott between infant and mother and, later, between patient and analyst; or, in Guattari's professional milieu, between patient and nurse, nurse and doctor, intern and doctor, etc. As the infant separates his or her mother from him/herself, s/he moves from the state of being merged with to being in a relation to her (Winnicott, 1971: 14–15). Indistinction is replaced by a space of signification as the mother is positioned as 'not-me' by the infant as opposed to a 'me-extension'. The mother, like the analyst, must adjust accordingly to this new relation with a willingness to let go. This shift from dependency to autonomy in the variable 'potential space' is for Winnicott paradoxical: it exists but cannot exist because infant and mother are joined and separated. If this paradoxicality is not tolerated, neither infant nor patient will have the opportunity to achieve personal autonomy. Tolerance is vital because what makes this space 'intermediate' is that its contents – objects representing the infant's or patient's transition – are neither assignable strictly speaking to psychic reality nor the actual world. To express this somewhat differently, a transitional object such as the mother's face is presented intermediately to the infant in such a way that s/he remains unaware that the s/he is not its creator.

The 'potential space' between is where reliability is manifested, that is, the mother's love and the analyst's involvement, and this reliability gives the infant or patient 'confidence' in what Winnicott calls the 'environmental factor' (Winnicott 1971: 102–3); confidence is felt on the basis of experience and will be different for every individual. How, then, does one create an environment of confidence in a psychiatric clinic?

The institutional object, like the transitional object, represents all the phenomena associated with contextualizing the psychotherapeutic cure and foregrounding the environment. The question of confidence is just as vital for Guattari (1972: 90–1) since it is this very environment which is problematic: 'psychiatric hospitals [like dual analyses undertaken in them] certainly provide us with the best example of "institutional objects" radically detoumed from their manifest social finality'. Despite themselves, psychiatric hospitals produce illness rather than treat it. The institutional object is known by means of group subjectivity, and the innovative conceptual tool used to pose the question is transversality. The foregrounding of the institutional context and the positing of this 'object', knowable through the subjectivity of the group, entails that the object plays a vitally important role in the life of such groups; just as the Lacanian *objet a* is the cause of the subject's – here, group's – desire and informs its fantasy life, the institutional object is what is real for these group subjects.

Subjectivity is a group phenomenon. It is completely deindividuated and depersonalized and ecologized, a consequence of foregrounding the social environment of the institution. There are different kinds of subjectivity, but they are always of the group. Subjectivity involves, then, non-predetermined interrelations, non-linear and non-logical 'evolution', and the production of differences. Remember this: if the part has priority over the whole, as it does for both Guattari and Deleuze, the whole cannot predetermine the future of the part. From Winnicott, Guattari also developed a sense of the between, the potential space. In his later collaborations with Deleuze, transversality is explicitly a creature of the middle. Guattari will eventually place the greatest emphasis on the potential as in virtual: it isn't contained in the actual and isn't constrained by typically dyadic frames (analyst–analysand; left and right banks). It is, rather, a space in which becomings are truly creative – radically open and simply not what is now actual. Near the end of his life Guattari will theorize along these lines a virtual ecology. Let's be patient. We still have a long way to go.

Coefficient of Transversality

In Guattari's early writings transversality is thought of in terms of a coefficient, a quantity theorized with the assistance of a therapeutic bestiary (horses, porcupines, flocks of birds and moulting animals, not to mention the creatures of the psychoanalytic bestiary) in terms of a degree of blindness or the wearing of adjustable blinkers by the members of the various groups in an institution. In my interpretation I have emphasized the bestiary over the connotations the concept has across mathematics, physics, thermodynamics, architecture, etc.[3] I take this approach because Guattari never carefully worked out its scientistic implications, leaving the labour of explication to his animals. He did suggest that the 'coefficient' he had in mind was from thermodynamics, although it was not one of performance, but that of entropy. Guattari (1972: 80–1) first asked his readers to imagine a group of interns among whom existed a great potential for transversal relations within the group and outside of it. As a group, interns normally have little real power. Their high level of transversality would remain latent to the extent that its institutional effects would be extremely limited. Despite the obvious import of social lines of force in this situation, Guattari proposed a thermodynamic comparison: 'one could say that the excessive institutional entropy of this state of transversality leads to the conduction or the encystment of every weak impulse to locally reduce it'. The transversality unavailable for affecting widespread institutional change actually increases by absorbing every hesitant or vague tendency to disturb it. This state of transversality seeks to return to its latency, that is, to maximize its entropy. It is certainly no easy task to find the group(s) that actually holds the key to 'regulating the latent transversality of the entire institution'; even those that appear weak may prove to be powerful. Guattari (1977: 247–8) later returned to the concept of the coefficient in the course of characterizing psychoanalysis as a politico-religious movement with a vested interest in the collective paranoia which it studies. He was fascinated by the character and functioning of such paranoia, and proposed to 'determine the nature of a *coefficient of collective paranoia*, a coefficient complementary and inverse to what I had proposed, about ten years ago, as the *coefficient of transversality*'. The latter is connective and communicative, and the former is restrictive and reticent.

Guattari likened the 'interpretation' of institutional entropy to transference, with the proviso that it was neither something established, analysed and dismantled on the way to a successful dual analysis, nor in the context of group analysis, was it something given by someone for this express purpose, individual or otherwise, by simply stepping into the role of 'analyser' (Guattari, 1972: 79). Although 'interpretation' may be given by anyone, even the 'imbecile of the ward', who makes him/herself heard at the right time, from which it follows that interpretation must be met halfway, which itself entails a peripatetic psychiatry that is not stuck behind a desk or a couch or even limited to one hospital ward – the 'psych' floor – it is still the analyst who must identify it as such; yet, this is not his/her exclusive prerogative. Even if the analyst does not hide behind a rigid hierarchical power relation in which the nurses do not communicate with him/her (they only take directions) but only with the patients, s/he cannot simply efface him/herself. The Master must allow him/herself to be displaced. The Master must assume responsibility for his/her actions and interpretations because they may stifle transversality. If the Master isn't displaced, what are the consequences? Well, s/he might mistakenly install him/herself as a superego model for the analysand; this renders transference onto the Master a common enough affair. While Lacan (1977: 246, 251) certainly struggled in his writings with the ethical error of this way, especially in his criticisms of British analysts who made the mistake of setting themselves up as model superegos with which their analysands should identify, it became grossly distorted in his cult following, according to Guattari. Guattari guarantees the renunciation of the exploitation of this position through the Master's displacement in the institutional hierarchy, while maintaining an empty locus for an emergent 'analyser' to occupy.

Guattari suggested the following of transversality: it may be low or high; it may be opened or restricted; it may be latent or manifest; it is homogeneous, even though different intensities exist here and there in the institution; it is a property of groups, and it is always present to some degree, just as the transference, as Freud once thought, was present from the outset of the analysis, in the somewhat banal sense that anyone who can libidinally cathect onto another person is engaged in intimate communication.

Let's consider Guattari's horses, which illustrate the coefficient of transversality:

> Imagine a fenced field in which there are horses wearing adjustable blinkers, and let's say that the 'coefficient of transversality' will be precisely the adjustment of the blinkers. If the horses are completely blind, a certain kind of traumatic encounter will be produced. As soon as the blinkers are opened, one can imagine that the horses will move about in a more harmonious way. (1972: 79)

Blinkers prevent transversal relations; they focus by severely circumscribing a visual field. The adjustment of them releases the existing, but blinkered, quantity of transversality. While horse blinkers are supposedly preventative – that is, they prevent a horse from being frightened or distracted – they may also cause a fright by their very restrictiveness. Indeed, the opening of them may initially produce less than harmonious relations; and, as for the harmony of group relations, they are certainly not guaranteed by the opening of blinkers. Transversality is the tool used to open hitherto closed logics and hierarchies. Guattari continues: 'Let's try to represent the manner in which people comport themselves in relation to one another from the affective point of view.' To put it bluntly, horseplay was commonplace in psychoanalysis. Guattari's choice of the blinkered horse is reminiscent of the example Freud used in *The Ego and the Id* (*SE* 19: Section II; and *New Introductory Lectures*, Lecture XXXI, *SE* 22) to explain what the ego is in relation to the id: 'like a man on horseback, who has to hold in check the superior strength of the horse; with this difference, that the rider tries to do so with his own strength while the ego uses borrowed forces'. The weakness of the ego (which also obtains in relation to the superego to which it is servile) is compensated by its tactical ingenuity in getting the horse to go where it wants, even if it must on occasion merely guide the horse along the way it wants to go. What Guattari leaves out of his analogy, among other things, is the person whose task it is to adjust the blinkers. Horses, like persons, can be broken, that is, the transversality of the groups in an institution can be destroyed by the rigid imperatives of management, nurses, doctors.

Guattari follows his shift from horses to persons by jumping from horses to porcupines: 'According to Schopenhauer's famous parable of the freezing porcupines, nobody can stand being too close to one's fellows.' Guattari is following the trail laid down by Freud in his *Group Psychology and the Analysis of the Ego* when he also quoted Schopenhauer to make the same point. The group is characterized, Freud thought, by the character of its libidinal ties. Both Guattari and Freud quote Schopenhauer:

> One cold winter's day, a company of porcupines huddled together to protect themselves against the cold by means of one another's warmth. But they were pricked by each other's quills, and it was not long before they drew apart again. The persistent cold drew them back together, but once again they felt the painful pricks. They alternately drew together and apart for some time until they discovered an acceptable distance at which they would be free of both evils. (Guattari, 1972: 60; Freud, *SE* 18: 101)

Presumably, a high coefficient of transversality does not straightforwardly produce harmonious group relations. The adjustment of the blinkers of patients by hospital officials, that is, from on high, or from below by an activist group of patients themselves, is likely to have little effect in traditional settings in which blindness is systematically deployed by an institution for its own ends because it is an effective way of maintaining the status quo, reinforcing its authority, and producing docile bodies through psychopharmacological 'adjustments'. Additionally, the parable of the porcupines is itself not dynamic enough to completely nip in the bud any incipient mythmaking about group togetherness, although Guattari was always critical of the utopian communities (the infamous households, the utopian therapeutic communities of the Philadelphia

Association headed by R. D. Laing, for example) favoured by British anti-psychiatrists.

Transversality is generally facilitated by opening and maximizing communication between the different levels of organization in an institution. At this point in his career Guattari was still working with the Freudian manifest–latent distinction. So, when he writes of the possibility of adjusting, that is, strengthening or weakening the coefficient of transversality, he immediately appeals to two different dimensions of communication: manifest and latent. Now, transversality is unconscious. What this means as a working principle is that the groups holding the real power (read latent) in the institution do not necessarily coincide with those groups who manifestly run the place (the clinic is really run by a particular group of patients or head nurse). This being the case, the levels of transversality in the groups with the real power 'unconsciously determines the adjustment of the extensive possibilities of other levels of transversality' (Guattari, 1972: 80). There isn't just one level of transversality but, rather, many levels and, moreover, openings at one level have effects at another. Guattari continued:

> The problem of the real relation of forces needs to be analysed: everyone knows that the law of the State is not made by the ministries. Similarly, in a psychiatric hospital it may happen that *de facto* power eludes the official representatives of the law only to be distributed among various subgroups: departments, big shots or – why not? – patients' clubs, staff associations, etc. (1972: 81)

The questions are who is in charge here and now, and who has the potential to take charge? Which group can occupy the 'potential space between'? On the level of the expression of reformist sentiments it is desirable, Guattari suggests, that the caregivers themselves, the doctors and nurses, 'control the factors capable of modifying the atmosphere, the relationships, the real running of the institution'. But an analysis based upon transversality does not accept the simple declaration of reforms for this still implies a vertical hierarchy as much as a dichotomy between internal reform and external militant agitation. Guattari was highly critical of reformist sentiments (every attempt at 'social adaptation') in the anti-psychiatry movement because they prevented fundamental change; indeed, innovations at the staff level tended to retreat into 'institutional interests' (Guattari, 1996b: 43). In every instance the militant analyst seeks the groups holding the real power. Holding power is not a static matter to be revealed once and for all: 'the subject of the institution, the effective – that is to say unconscious – subject, is never given once and for all. It has to be flushed out' (Guattari, 1972: 81).

All of this has a rather explicit Freudian ring to it (and as we will see with regard to Guattari's later recoding of psychoanalytic categories and topographies onto ontological dimensions, there is a persistent psychoanalytic shadow hanging over everything): the introduction of transversality in the group is like Freud's introduction of 'a new class of psychical material', the latent dream-thoughts, thus necessitating the investigation of the relation, through the processes of the dream work, between the manifest content of dreams and the latent dream thoughts. The meaning of a dream must be 'disentangled', just as the group holding the real power must be similarly 'flushed out'.

Is transversality horizontal or vertical or both? It is anti-top down, organizationally speaking, and not purely horizontal. Taken individually, these orientations are impasses; taken together, they are blinkers. Both must be swept away. You can't solve problems on the ward by issuing official directives from on high; and you can't hide issues in the horizontal drift across a single plane.

Theory of Groups

Guattari's non-absolute distinction between two kinds of group subjects, subjugated groups and subject groups, is maintained by appeals to the difference between the ability to make a statement (subject group) as opposed to having one's cause heard but without verification of it; the subject group's alienation has an internal source arising from its efforts to connect with other groups, thus exposing its members, risking their security, responding with collective paranoia and neurotic obsessions; whereas the subjugated group's alienation is thought to have an external source, from which it protects itself by withdrawing into itself and constructing richly paranoid protective formations, providing a kind of refuge and a distorted sense of security for its members. The manifest–latent distinction is employed to indicate that the unconscious desire of the group 'needs to be decoded through an interpretation of the diverse ruptures of meaning arising in the phenomenal order' (Guattari, 1972: 76). As I mentioned earlier, this sort of group analysis does not attempt to grasp the 'static truth' (a universal) of a particular range of symptoms. Indeed, the analytic goal of the modification of the different coefficients of transversality existing in and among the groups in an institution cannot be said to be aligned with 'group engineering' or 'role adaptation', even though Guattari explicitly described how the 'strengthening of an existing level of transversality in an institution allows a new kind of dialogue to establish itself in the group', thus enabling a patient to use the group 'in the manner of a mirror', Guattari specified, in order to manifest hitherto repressed aspects of both the group and him/herself; this gives one a 'collective mode of expression'. The patient's joining of a subject group, functioning in the manner of a 'pure signifying chain', allows him/her to 'reveal him/herself to him/herself beyond his/her imaginary and neurotic impasses' (Guattari, 1972: 82); whereas, if a neurotic or psychotic were to join a subjugated group, s/he would have his/her narcissism reinforced or find a place that would accommodate the silent exploration of his/her passions. And there is a certain freedom in this. Let's not label one group good and the other bad.

A few points of clarification are required. Guattari sought, in other words, to make room for the emergence of interpretation in its singularity and irreducibility to making sense: 'The silence of a catatonic can make up a part, perhaps even constitute the masterpiece, of an institutional assemblage of enunciation', as he later remarked in an interview (Guattari, 1996b: 137). The joining of a subject group enables a patient to become a signifier in a communication system whose members are interdependent, yet simultaneously in a relation of difference, but nonetheless totally involved in a collective process which frees one from the individuated hell of isolation. The use of the group as a mirror suggests that the patient can minimally perceive others like him/herself, and is in this way drawn into an intersubjective relation; such a relation is not, however, dual in the sense that Lacan attached to the phantasies of the imaginary register (where all such mirror phenomena are placed) in which the subject finds that s/he is another, the mirror image alienating him/her from him/herself, as if s/he is captured by it. A signifying chain is not conceived of as a straight line (Lacan's rejection of the linearity of the signifier, 1977: 154), and not even a coil, but as a series of layered, ever-widening loops, linked with other such loops (Lacan's rings of a necklace that are themselves rings in other necklaces made of rings, 1977: 153) with vertical and horizontal dependencies (value and signification), as well as the fundamental structures of association (metaphor and metonymy). To use the group as a mirror is to experience oneself as a group subject.

Guattari's two kinds of groups are modelled on Sartre's distinction between serial being and the group in fusion. Concerning this legacy he has written in an essay 'La Borde: A Clinic Unlike Any Other', collected under the title of *Chaosophy*:

> A word that was fashionable then was 'seriality', which defined, according to Jean-Paul Sartre, the repetitive and empty character of a mode of existence arising from the way a practico-inert group functioned. (Guattari, 1995b: 191)

The members of a series are united in being turned towards an exterior object in which they have an interest, embodying a prior praxis without having a project in common of which they are aware and, indeed, without really being aware of one another. Guattari was deeply interested in how to move a group out of serial being, and this definition corresponds to what he called a subjugated group. The subjugated group's unity lies, then, outside itself; the nurses appearing each day to administer medications unite the inidividuals on award, but in their separateness, because their practico-inert being is determined by the psychopharmacological imperatives of the institution. The nurse is an agent of a practico-inert structure, and to resist his/her requires an enormous effort of critique of the reasonableness and efficacy of the behaviours s/he presupposes, both of the patient, him/herself, the doctors, the medical schools, the drug industries, etc.

Guattari wasn't merely attracted by a fashionable concept. The Sartrean legacy touched him quite deeply. One cannot help but notice the emotional texture of his references to the scapegoating of Sartre during the public acrimony over his novel *Nausea* and media hysteria regarding suicide rates among French youth (Guattari, 1996b: 72), or the value and influence of Sartre as his model of a reflective, militant intellectual (1996b: 121); the restrictiveness of Sartre's vision is duly noted as well, with reference to 'Saint' Jean Genet (1996b: 218). Indeed, the list goes on and on. Perhaps the most telling testimony was embedded in Guattari's reflections from 1966:

> Another of my benefactors was Sartre. It is not an easy admission to make. I like Sartre not so much for the coherence of his theoretical work but, on the contrary, for all his zigzags, all his errors, for all of his good faith about his mistakes, from 'Les Communistes' and *Nausea* to his attempts at integrating Marxian dialectics into mainstream philosophical thought, an attempt that surely failed. I like Sartre because of his failure; it seems to me that he positioned himself transversally in relation to the contradictory demands that tormented him but which he never let go; he solved no problem, with the exception of never succumbing to the elegance of structuralism or the dogmatic certainties of several distinguished adherents of Maoism. (1972: 154–5)

In an otherwise highly charged dialogue staged by Constantin Boundas (1993: 32–43) between Sartre and Deleuze, the microscopic attention paid to what emerges as the central contrastive point, the structure of alterity, erases any trace of Guattari. This is especially evident in the passing mentions of the theory of groups, but no less telling when Sartre's so-called 'confusions' about the structure of alterity are firmly placed on the shoulders of the subject/object dialectic, in opposition to Deleuze's foreclosure of the Other that reaches beyond both subjectivity and alterity. Guattari, Deleuze and Boundas have in their own ways appreciated the lessons of Sartre's confusions. It makes a great deal of difference whether these confusions are valued for their political or phenomenological lessons, especially since the latter may themselves contextually 'bracket' or foreclose the former in a manner that abstracts the staged dialogue from its practical setting – the street, the clinic, the self-protective *groupuscule*. I do not wish to accommodate the dialectic. I want to underline Guattari's appreciation of Sartre's confusions on emotional and political bases, and to find in them a force that animates the best in Guattari's political dialogues with Negri and others: the feeling and admission of failure; confusion on the part of a generation of defeated radicals; the personal effects of the disintegration of movements and relationships; the effects of aging on one's vision of a militant social practice, of trying to reanimate widely discredited movements in the face of monumental transformations, the maturing of a new generation and the ripening of intergenerational strife; the experience of prison, of harassment by the state and the media; of the passing of one's cherished interlocutors, etc.

The subject group is a kind of group in fusion that has liquidated its seriality and come together in 'the flash of a common praxis', in mutual reciprocity rather than mutual Otherness, but still united in the first instance in virtue of a common object defined in Sartrean terms as external (Sartre, 1976: 253ff.). The distinction is non-absolute, and a subject group can easily decay into a subjugated group; the latter 'inert gathering with its structure of seriality is the basic type of sociality', according to Sartre (1976: 348). The movement in Sartrean dialectical sociology from collectives to groups, from serial being to groups-in-fusion, from subjugated to subject groups, registers the presence or absence of the source of unity: it is either here or there. Hence, the subject group has interiorized its external source of unity and made of it a common objective, refining and restructuring it along the way. This negation of an external negation (not a common praxis defined from the outside but the negation of this) takes place in specific material circumstances and entails that the praxis of one member is the common action of everyone in the group: my praxis is yours, too. Importantly, the results of this totalized understanding must be continually interiorized if the group is not to decay back into seriality. The failure to fully liquidate seriality amounts to the equivalence of subject and subjugated groups.

Any reader of Guattari's essay on transversality may also notice that he very early on introduced a passage from Freud's late essay (originally 1933) 'Anxiety and the Instinctual Life', from the *New Introductory Lectures* (*SE* 22), in which the distinction between anxiety produced by an internal as opposed to an external danger must have had some bearing on his reading of the sources of alienation in the two kinds of group subjects. More specifically, Freud maintained that there are determinants of anxiety appropriate to every developmental phase (i.e. castration in the phallic phase), but that these are never completely dropped. Guattari seized upon castration – which Freud went to some length to justify as a real, external danger – as a key to social relations in advanced capitalist and socialist bureaucratic societies: there is no end to its threat, under various guises. Guattari (1972: 74) considered castration to be a *'supplementary term* in the situational triangulation of the Oedipus complex, so that we will never finish with this threat which will permanently reactivate what Freud called "an unconscious need for punishment"'. The logic of this supplement is that, understood as a 'social reality', the need for punishment will be blindly repeated. Its basis is in an 'irrational morality', Guattari specified, since it cannot be articulated as an 'ethical legality': irrational to be sure, and a 'danger' belonging to the signifying logic of contemporary society. The threat of punishment plays, then, a regulatory role: it is blind but socially effective. What is regulated is desire.

If the castration complex is never satisfactorily resolved, and the need for punishment is endlessly repeated, it follows that the superego's growth will be stunted and the ego will be sacrificed on the altar of the mystifications of so-called great leaders who are at once fathers–kings–gods, and whose abilities to actually intervene in 'the signifying machine of the economic system' were never very great, anyway, even though they were and are commonly and 'collectively pseudo-phallicized' by voters and the party faithful. It is the castration complex that compels the little boy to give up his incestual attachments to mummy and ambivalence towards daddy, and with the threat of castration the superego is born, and thus daddy's injunction to stop playing with yourself is forever perpetuated, and forever triggered by desire, which cannot be separated from repression. With little girls things are, as Freud tried to have it, quite different because the threat of castration does nothing to demolish the Oedipus complex and the girl has no incentive to develop a superego akin to her brother's. Freud mused that the formation of the little girl's superego is impaired. Of course, Freud changed his mind about the parallel between boys and girls several times, until he decided to change the order of the

Oedipus and castration complexes: with girls the castration complex comes first and precipitates the Oedipus complex. The girl doesn't have, so the story goes, any of the smashed bits of the Oedipus complex with which to fashion a cruel superego for herself. The point of this diversion into Freud's fabulations is to show that Guattari (1972: 75) believed that the analyst must attend very carefully to the 'goal of modifying the objects "incorporated" by the superego, transmuting such objects in a sort of new "intitiatic" reception, clearing from its path the blind social demand of a certain castrative procedure to the exclusion of all else'. Why should parental threats be constantly repeated as if life was an interminable drama of the threat of persecution for our desires?

Indeed, why should the mythic threats of psychoanalysis be constantly repeated as if life was an interminable analysis? Guattari is seeking nothing less than a way to limit the effects of the legacy of castration in the superego's hold over desire.

In an interview from 1973, Guattari (1995b: 214–15) remarked of Freud's final reflections on the castration complex in men and women in his 'Analysis Terminable and Interminable' (*SE* 23) that it rests on familialism (the heterosexual family and even the cancellation of homosexual desire in the struggles of men against a passive or 'feminine' attitude towards other men) and phallocentrism (women's penis envy and the need to convert it into a normative heterosexual desire for a child). Guattari points out that psychoanalysis runs up against the final barrier of men who cannot master their castration-anxiety because they refuse to acknowledge that there may be times when they have to adopt a passive attitude towards other men (they cannot accept being cured by another man) and women who cannot acknowledge their lack of a penis and, thus, their anatomical destiny, and as a result become depressed, and, worst of all for the economy of psychoanalysis, cease to believe in a cure. Feminist scholars have made much of this Freudian shipwreck on the reef of castration, turning to Lacan's structural version of psychoanalysis for a way out (Gallop, 1985: 20; Ragland-Sullivan, 1991: 57). In *Anti-Oedipus* what is lamented is 'resignation to Oedipus, to castration' that accompanies the introduction of lack into desire. In short, 'psychoanalysis castrates the unconscious' from which it requires belief rather than production (Deleuze and Guattari, 1977:

59–60). The modification of 'introjects' of the superego stripped of their familialism (every desire mediated by mummy–daddy) and breaking the exclusivity of the mythical phallus in determinations of the common lot of the sexes, what Guattari referred to as its 'initiatic' reception such that the superego would open itself, would 'admit' something new, in the same manner as blinkers are opened (the blindness motif is a psychoanalytic symbol for castration, anyway), entails that desire no longer triggers repression. Psychoanalysis is, as Guattari once called it, 'the best capitalist drug': it's legal in most places and, you can get off on its ritual interpretations and how it makes desire a family affair, shutting the door of consulting rooms on the social. And its fixation on the superego, indelibly stamped by daddy's authority, means that all through life desire is crushed by the injunctions and prohibitions of the same castrating daddy requiring either that desire should desire its own repression or burn itself out with guilt by resisting repression: in school, in church, in politics, in the doctor's office, during visits with your mummy, and especially in the consulting room. How does Guattari modify and transmute the objects incorporated by the superego without setting off repression? He explains in an interview 'The Best Capitalist Drug':

> About ten years ago [circa 1963] I introduced the notion of *transversality* to express the capacity of an institution to remodel the ways of access it offers the superego so that certain symptoms and inhibitions are removed. Modification of the latent coefficient of transversality implies the existence of an erotic focal point, a group Eros, and a take-over – even if partial – of local politics by a group-subject. A social formation can modify the erotic 'causality' which sets off the activity of the superego. This modification of the ways it accommodates the superego leads to a radical transformation of the whole of the [Freudian] topography. (Guattari 1995b: 215)

The superego overcodes desire with repression and persecution in the name of the father. Resignation invades desire; the best a man can hope for is to take his place in the great chain of daddies, cold and remote, like a superego. Guattari concerns himself with desire in the group, a group Eros that does not belong to an individual ego but is a larger formation that cannot be represented through the intermediaries of the family. Indeed, individuals in subjugated groups live and/or phantasize their group belonging by means of subjugation (Oedipus and castration): the head doctor, the nurse, the intern, the janitor are all daddy (Deleuze and Guattari, 1977: 64). Transversality has the task of ensuring that the institution doesn't produce Oedipalizable objects through its routines and representatives, and that the potential middle is opened.

How to Get Out from Behind the Couch

Guattari (1972: 83) wondered 'how can the head doctor be convinced to accept and even solicit questions about his actions, without having him recoil before the panic fear of being torn to bits?' The doctor's acceptance of this questioning, his/her 'assumption of the phantasm of breaking apart . . . plays an essential role in the setting up of a structure of transversality' and the modification of the objects incorporated by the superegos of the patients (and, indeed, of the doctor as well). This assumption puts the doctor into direct contact with the phantasms of the group, and enables the group to learn a new role, and to question and redefine old roles. It is through this process that the aforementioned 'initiatic' acceptance of new objects by the superego may be brought about, primarily by setting up ideals which directly affect what the superego incorporates; castration doesn't evaporate but, instead, it is 'articulated with social demands different from those that the patients have previously known in their familial, professional and other relations' (Guattari, 1972: 83). The castration complex may be, then, modified according to local conditions involving new organizations (patients' clubs) and access to new media (plastic arts) affording opportunities for resingularization through the opening of new Universes of reference to hitherto unartistic persons. When the head doctor relinquishes for a time, for instance, his/her privileges by participating in the various groups of the institution, in the course of which s/he takes up a variety of different responsibilities, this redefinition of roles contributes to the erosion of the head doctor's social status and the 'alienation phantasy' underlying it, as well as having widespread repercussions in the institution (Guattari, 1972: 83). Transversality is fundamentally and radically social and political and in addition its implementation requires a great deal of courage and trust on the part of everyone concerned; it is also extremely local, involving a local politics, that of the subject group acquiring enough power to be capable of formulating a goal and trying to achieve it; a group of doctors willing to risk their exalted status. But the modification of the objects incorporated by the superego requires nothing less than a very high level of experimentation irreducible to experiments by the staff themselves. Remember Deleuze and Guattari's (1977: 67) admission from *Anti-Oedipus*: 'We are not saying that Oedipus and castration do not amount to anything.'

Every local context must be appreciated. This is precisely the role that Guattari sought to play in his work at La Borde through what was called *la grille* (the grid): the schedule of rotating tasks undertaken by medical and support staff, which were overseen by a supervisor whose role was to deal with all the practical difficulties, in concert with the founding and organization of patients' clubs (by Guattari himself) which enjoyed a certain financial and adminstrative autonomy from the institution and had real means to achieve their self-directed goals, themselves not confined to the inside. The origin of these clubs, in France at least, dates from the Second World War and the decisive influence of the 'red psychiatrist' François Tosquelles at the clinic of St Alban. The patients' clubs were the institutional means for the formation of subject groups to the extent that they were founded, operated and directed by patients, even if, ultimately, they were overseen by the institution. Valorizations of the horizontality of such clubs and the array of intra-hospital organizations that mark the history of hospital reform in France miss the point that transversality is not realized by unidimensional accomplishments. The goals of these experimental activities were multiple, for not only was a transversal structure set up to enable a certain reciprocity to prevail between groups hitherto divided hierarchically, but to create an atmosphere in which hitherto repressed phantasies could come to light; not to mention that new encounters with different institutionally based matters of expression (the head physician working in the kitchen, and the kitchen staff working on the newspaper) were facilitated by the desegregation of roles, breaking the grip of routine and boredom with the opportunity for improvisation and innovation. None of this guaranteed, it should be said, warm, fuzzy group togetherness. In fact, while it was not too difficult to get the medical staff to take up such tasks as dishwashing, cleaning and cooking, it was much more difficult, and often proved impossible, to get non-medical staff to care for patients (so, compatible tasks were found). The compromises were many, the fears were great; the very need to find compatible tasks for non-medical staff speaks strongly to the limits of experimentation in the grid. But the idea of rotating tasks really did require the physicians and the non-medical staff to adopt quite different points of view. It required a militant commitment to institutional critique and, to the credit of Guattari and his colleagues, a great deal of personal courage to abandon the well-established posture of the distant, untouchable doctor–teacher–professor. Indeed, as Guattari's close colleague, and in some ways mentor from a young age, Jean Oury once said of the grid: 'This is more important than the ravings of pseudo-intellectuals who have never picked up a broom!' (Oury *et al*., 1977: 20). Constant questioning is risky for where there are reassurances there are also obsessional defence mechanisms, which explains why castration is not just easily theorized away as some psychoanalytic hobbyhorse.

Within the system of work rotation, however, compatible tasks were neither easily found nor managed. Guattari (1977: 166–7) once described how the emergence of a leader – a tyrannical cook with a strong sense of territory in the kitchen at La Borde – constituted a social and institutional knot that needed to be untied. This sense of knot is not borrowed from Lacanian topology but, rather, from Laing, despite Guattari's (1996b: 40) criticisms of the mirror games of the latter's familialistically tinged poetry. The cook's tyranny over the kitchen is irreducible to its familial underpinnings as well as static decodings of the oppressive power relations resulting from inter-individual manoeuvring and temporary micro-sociological constellations. Knots such as these, to the extent that they tie up the work rotation, 'can appear inescapable at an elementary micro-sociological level [but] are perhaps no longer so in a living institutional structure' (Guattari, 1977: 167). A dynamic conception of the institution requires the placement of the knot in relation to the institution and the latter in its social context (government supervision, suppliers and other clinics, Guattari notes), the leader's relation to the transitory group hierarchies, and his/her conception of the social relations for which s/he militates. The cook's refusal to allow free access to the kitchen, Guattari writes,

> is inseparable from the government officials who supervise the clinic as well as the repressive phantasms which crystallize the roles, functions and alienating modes of the division of labour, as much at the level of technical services as treatments. All the desiring machines relating to eating, with preparing and providing nourishment are, in this way, more or less blocked. (Guattari, 1977: 168)

How, then, does some 'authority' intervene without exacerbating the sadomasochistic relation to authority of the cook? The goal, Guattari contends, is to ' "turn" the symptom "leadership" to the profit of a more "constructive" and satisfactory drive'. The failure to follow the lead of desire no matter where it leads in order to find a place at which the cook's desiring-machine can communicate with the alimentary machines of the patients and staff will only result in a kind of 'turning' that distorts and adapts desire to a more useful, that is, normal role (making ergotherapy in the kitchen function at whatever cost), which Guattari wanted to avoid.

While we are on the subjects of cooks, it is instructive to consider another of Guattari's anecdotal reflections about life at La Borde. In the course of an interview from the mid-1980s, he remarked:

> In a period of time in which everyone was very unhappy, an event sprang forth which, without being able to know precisely why, changed the atmosphere. An unexpected process led to the secretion of different universes of reference; one sees things otherwise. Not only does the subjectivity change, but equally the fields of possibility change, the life projects. For example, a cook, originally from the Ivory Coast, decided to return there. However, he had no means to establish himself again in his village. He worked at La Borde for a number of years and was much loved. A group formed to help him, which transformed itself into an association in accord with the law of 1901: La Borde-Ivoire. They collected twenty thousand francs to assist him in his move. Later a doctor and a nurse went to visit him.

Then, in turn, a kind of village came to visit La Borde for three months. Now there is a group of six patients who are going there for three weeks of vacation. Here we have a *process of institutional singularization*. Is this psycho-therapy? Good works? Militancy? In each case the local subjectivity was profoundly modified, especially its latent racism. (1996b: 128–9)

Although this description engages Guattari's later emphasis on subjectification and singularization, it illustrates the transformative effects of the work of a subject group (formed under a French law dating from 1 July 1901 permitting anyone to form a group with a specific social goal) on the transversal resonances of existential fields of reference, specifically the colour of the cook's skin and the meaning of the Ivory Coast in a racist group phantasy. Of course, by the 1970s Guattari had explicitly theorized the accommodation afforded to regressive phenomena in a generative schizoanalysis and their modification in a transformational pragmatics. Whether this was the aforementioned tyrannical cook is unimportant. The example sheds some much-needed light on why patients in French psychiatric facilities, unlike those incarcerated across North America, can form associations and work towards goals outside the institution. Typically, psychiatric inmates in North America are stripped of their rights, and this has informed the shape of the anti-psychiatric struggle over there, putting a great deal of emphasis on human rights. In France, the formation of subject groups has a legal foundation to build upon.

Reflecting on his own experience in a variety of militant organizations (youth and party) in the 1950s in another important early essay 'The Group and the Person', Guattari remarked that regardless of whether or not the groups actually had any real effect, the important thing was, rather, that 'certain types of action and concentration represented a break with habitual social processes and, above all, a rupture with the modes of communication and emotional demonstration inherited from the family' (Guattari, 1972: 156). This rupture was critical for distinguishing between subject and what Guattari sometimes called, echoing Sartre, 'object' groups (corresponding to subjugated groups, but employed by Sartre [1976: 371–2] to indicate the totality of a group of persons constituted as an object insofar as I see it and it influences my course of action, as opposed to a group-subject, which I totalize without ever seeing, but on the basis that it sees me, making me its object, and threatening my freedom), and in addition presented 'a minimal possibility of taking hold of the desire of the group . . . and a possibility of escaping from the immutable determinisms whose models are furthered by the structure of the nuclear family, the organization of labour in industrial societies (in terms of wages and hierarchies), the Army, the Church, the University'; in Freud's group psychology, one may recall, the Church and the Army served him as primary examples of complex, artificial groups with leaders which furthered his characterization of the group by the libidinal ties between its members and with its leader(s), that is, horizontal and vertical relations. For Guattari, the same leader can participate in both kinds of groups.

Clearly, then, transversality was a key element of a militant practice aiming at a rupture with inherited models of organization. To transversalize the organization of a given institution is a creative act giving rise to subject groups capable of internally generating and directing their own projects, ensuring that organization remains close to the groups themselves, while simultaneously avoiding the slide into bureaucratic sclerosis; in diagramming the 'Leninist rupture' and the rise of the molar dictatorship of Stalin, for example, Guattari (1972: 159) suggested that the most excessive repressive measures were required to equal and exceed the 'richest current of social expression history has known'. Militants are often condemned to the phantasms of subjugated groups (the infantile disorders of ultra-leftism) which keep them from exploring the 'real texture of an organization'; they get hung up on the significations produced by the leadership rather than producing their own signifiers and speaking in the name of the institutions they create adequate to the course of their actions (not a party and its lines and programme for these are 'machines of repression producing antiproduction, that is, signifiers which plug and prohibit the emergence of all subjective expressions of the group'). Similarly, even subject groups may become bewitched by their own phantasies, losing their sense of direction for a time; these phantasies are transitional, however, and correspond to changes inside the group, rather than those requiring the subordination of the group (Guattari, 1972: 167). In *Anti-Oedipus* (Deleuze and Guattari, 1977: 348–9) the discussion of this point emphasized the mutual imbrication of the groups while maintaining the distinction between real, non-hierarchical coefficients of transversality and symbolic structures of subjugation, using the language of opening and closing to thread the subject–subjugated distinction through the fabric of desiring-production.

Institutional innovations such as 'the grid' put into place by Guattari and his colleagues at La Borde constituted a break with habit and routine that laid the groundwork for an 'intitiatic' reception and representation by the superego of new institutional objects and social relations. The transformation and diversification of routine and the presentation of real opportunities; the transversalization of hierarchy and the demonstration of the mutability of inherited models (from the family and the division of labour, to the irreducibility of the subject group to an individual delegated to interpret the situation, although I have suggested that certain tensions persist around this theme); the opportunity for active participation in social affairs: all of these breaks and ruptures formed an integral part of what Guattari characterized by the term 'initiatic'. Guattari's sense of 'initiation' is less anthropological than fundamentally autobiographical and tied to a militant practice; yet, for this reason, it is no less social. Morever, 'initiation' equally concerns how institutions are represented in the phantasies of groups.

In reflecting on his experiences in radical groups of various sorts, Guattari did not emphasize their effectiveness. Rather, he emphasized their 'initiatic' value in the sense ascribed above to 'the grid'. Significantly, Guattari's experience of militancy gave him a creative edge in his dealings with institutions; they acquired 'a sort of plasticity, at least at the level of representation in the intentional field' (1972: 157). The revolutionary and institutional creativity of subject groups can be stifled and crushed when the links between their organizations and projects are broken. Guattari's example is the legacy of Stalin. What happens when this link is broken? The group closes in on itself and gets caught up in its own phantasmatic representations of its own organization:

the revolutionary organization has become detached from the signifier of the discourse of the working class to the profit of a totalization closed in on itself and antagonistic to the expression of the subjectivity of different sub-ensembles and groups, of these subject groups of which Marx spoke. Group subjectivity has no other means to express itself except in a phantasmatization which confines it to the sphere of the imaginary. (1972: 160–1)

'Breakthrough groups' decay into subjugated groups in this manner. The psycho-socio-political question is how to break from this imaginary (which can consist of no end of oddities from fascist delusions to theoretical noodling) and get back to the exploration of the 'real texture of an organization', as Guattari put it. The break, then, makes it impossible for a subject group to creatively (re)produce institutions.

Astute readers will have noticed Guattari's clever misreading of a quotation from Marx's 'Introduction' to the *Grundrisse* (1973: 86): 'Lastly, production also is not only a particular production. Rather, it is always a certain social body, a social subject, which is active in a greater or sparser totality of branches of production.' Guattari moves from the social subject to the subject group via 'a correlate of phantasmatization, with an element of social creationism that I tried to schematize in "transversality"' (Guattari, 1972: 154), as he put it. Social creativity, especially that of subject groups in relation to institutions, is moulded by the group phantasies delivered through modem initiations (various forms of apprenticeship, bourgeois phantasies of the university, failure neuroses of the Left) into dominant institutions. It would be incorrect to strictly separate phantasy from reality because the texture of an organization is composed of imaginary mechanisms. These subjective phenomena, however, are irreducible both to individuals and to manifest conditions (like soldiers marching back and forth in a square, or students lining up to register for their classes). Guattari's intentionally provocative transversalization of the Marxist social subject is at the expense of the inability of the workers' movement to grasp group phenomena (it's not their fault, really, Guattari adds, we are all at fault, because we rely on the wrong indicators). As I indicated above, Guattari's (1972: 163) bestiary explains the transversality of the group; here, he uses the image of a migrating flock of birds to suggest what is wrong with trying to explain the group belonging rationally, or individually, or in relation to official dictates, or manifest events in general: 'it has its own structure, shape, function, and course, all of which are determined without a meeting of the central committee, nor the elaboration of the party line!' While this image of the migrating flock overdetermines group coordination and togetherness, it serves Guattari as a foil for the inadequacies of the social theories of groups and the woodenness of political bureaucracies. But it is not only a foil: it also provides him with a way to underline how a group suddenly coalesces when it finds someone or thing upon which to hang a hitherto latent phantasy, what Guattari called an 'imaginary territorialization, a phantasmatic corporealization of the group which enfleshes subjectivity' (1972: 164).

Guattari always turned his therapeutics, at times rather vulgar if one thinks of parapraxes as the easiest pickings of psychopathology, to political ends with great mischief and delight. Consider his inflammatory 1970 essay 'The Maso-Maoists and the Impossible May' (1972), which hangs on what Freud called a 'political misprint'. Quoting the *Cahiers de la Gauche prolétarienne*, Guattari points out a typesetting error that rendered the G.P.'s recognition of the supposed 'universality and French reality' of Maoism into a politics lacking reality in France; 'la reconnaissance à travers la G.P. du maoïsme dans son universalité et sans [instead of dans] sa réalité en France' (1972: 276). Guattari even beseeched his comrade typesetter at *L'Idiot international* not to correct the typo he was exposing and to remain calm. This taunt led Guattari, who duly notes the erratum slip provided by the *Cahiers*, as well as the G.P.'s refusal of Freudianism, to use both of these as evidence that a lesson was under way about parapraxes, unwittingly sponsored by the G.P. itself. One cannot but knowingly exclaim: *traduttore*, *traditore*!

Transversality in the Later Guattari

I would now like to place Guattari's early elaboration of transversality in the context of the development of his thought by jumping ahead to his final published work, *Chaosmosis* (1995a). I need only remind the reader of a series of modifications that have taken place in his relationship to psychoanalysis. Consider, then, Guattari's first essay in the book, 'On the Production of Subjectivity'. Guattari's transversalist conception of subjectivity escapes the individual–social distinction as well as the givenness or preformedness of the subject either as a person or individual; subjectivity is both collective and auto-producing. *Chaosmosis* is full of refrains of Guattari's thought: his criticism of linguistic semiology and structuralism in the name of a-signifying phenomena; a rejection of Freudian psychogenetic stages of development in favour of a polyphonic conception of subjectivity of coexisting levels. These points are rather complex and I will not return to them in this essay. Suffice to say that I simply wish to note that Guattari favoured what he referred to as 'pragmatic applications' of structuralism; one such manifestation was the psychoanalytic theory of partial objects, especially the Lacanian theory of the *objet a*, which Guattari at times read through Bakhtin, especially as it concerned the autonomization of subjectivity in relation to aesthetic objects, the so-called 'partial enunciators': these are the references (objects) by means of which subjectivity enunciates itself (Guattari, 1995a: 13). A transversal conception of subjectivity entails the connection and embodiment in an assemblage of these partial–objects–enunciators. It is fair to say that the one specific thing Guattari held onto from his Lacanian training was the theorization of the partial object as the *objet a*. Transversality was worked through this Lacanian concept because it served, in Guattari's aforementioned early paper 'The Transference', to critique the dual analysis (the mother–child relation is triangular to the extent that there is a third detachable, displaceable object at issue – hair or, even better, the mother's love [Lacan, 1977: 197–8]). Lacanian, Kleinian and Winnicottian partial objects were all put into service, at one time or another by Guattari, even if their psychoanalytic specificity was challenged in the process; everybody remembers how, in *Anti-Oedipus*, Kleinian part objects were detached from their missing wholes and given interest, partiality, that is, as partial objects not subject to any exclusions. Eugene Holland (1988: 61) has shown that the schizoanalyst cuts Lacan's (1977: 193–4) L-schema of the psyche in two; only the top relation between the subject of speech *S* and his/her partial objects is retained, and the bottom relation between the ego, or what of the subject is reflected by his/her objects, and the Other, upon whose discourse the subject depends, is refused; that is, the Imaginary and Symbolic relations are discarded for the sake of the contact of the schizo subject's desire with its partial objects in the Real. It needs to be mentioned, not as a corrective to Holland but, rather, harkening back to the early papers of Guattari, that this was not yet the case, for the redefinition of roles, especially of the chief doctor, situates him/her on the symbolic plane and 'his/her role, now "articulated like a language", will find itself in direct contact with all the signifiers and phantasms of the group' (Guattari, 1972: 83). What this entails is that the grid is inscribed in the symbolic by means of a multiple semiotics (scriptural, gestural, etc.) and that the unconscious transversality that it releases is structured like a language. Lacan's topography of the unconscious was, of course, structural-linguistic. In other words, the early Guattari could not have done without the symbolic register. What Holland suggests, however, is that the pre-personological and the post-subject is invoked so as to evade the traps that come along with entry into the symbolic as well as the mirror games and impasses, not to mention the individuated organization, of a typically psychoanalytic imaginary.

Reflecting on his essay on transversality some years after its initial publication, Guattari (1977: 168–9) noted: 'I still accepted that certain techniques could, as such, contribute to the modification of what I then called "objects incorporated by the superego".' It incorrectly appeared as if there was 'on one side a superego, set in a person, and on the other side, a social context which interacts with it'. The institutional technique of work rotation was unfortunately applied in a rather mechanical way to the modification of the institutional objects, leaving the impression that the transversal analysis of the unconscious concerned individuals. Guattari did not want to leave the impression that such an analysis was psychologistic and personological. He additionally underlined that the institutional techniques developed at La Borde were themselves only as effective as the 'collective project which sustains them, the collective assemblage in the midst of which they are placed, is itself articulated in a micropolitics of desire relative to a much greater social field' (1977: 169).

The partial object survived Guattari's turn against his own analyst and was generalized into an ethico-aesthetic theory of the subjectification that escaped the shackles of personological, familial and structural linguistic models. There is a more or less direct link between the militant's ability to modify the institutional objects and conditions towards their new initiatic acceptance and the production of a kind of subjectivity that is not stunted by institutions under the sway of capital, for instance, which produces serial and elitist forms of subjectivity. Partial subjectification became a key part of a transversalist conception of the relation between, to adopt the language of Hjelmslevian glossematics as Guattari understood it, expression and content planes; the transversal relation at the level of form is between the phonemic system and semantic unities. But this initial relation was still too linguistic for Guattari. This struggle against linguistic imperialism was felt in many fields (see Genosko, 1998b: 175–90). Guattari then envisaged a critique of the formation of matter into semiotic substance such that substance would be shattered with the transversal relation between enunciative substances of a linguistic nature and non-semiotically formed matter; between, then, the linguistic and the machinic orders, whose relation would constitute machinic assemblages of enunciation. His guiding idea was to describe form– matter relations that skirted the category of substance, on both the planes of expression and content, and to christen these a-signifying semiotics, as a way out of glottocentric semiology, and a move towards the urging along and mapping-out of these creative subjectifications as they come into existence, embodying themselves in existential territories as they, to quote Guattari (1995a: 28), 'extract complex forms from chaotic material'.

Guattari's interest in the production of subjectivity required a new model – actually a metamodelization, in the wake of such crises of existing 'grand', scientistic modelizations affecting the relevancy of psychoanalysis, structuralism, marxism, etc., of the unconscious, beyond the work of both Freud and Lacan, loosened from 'tradition and invariancy', that is, the objective truths of the psyche. Guattari became, then, a forward-looking cartographer of the unconscious, a pragmatist whose formations centred on assemblages of subjectification, rather than a backward-looking scientific interpreter of a restricted topography all of whose roads led back to childhood or, for that matter, to the signifying chain:

Gilles Deleuze and I have similarly refused the Conscious–Unconscious dualism of the Freudian issues, and all the Manicheanist oppositions that follow on the level of oedipal triangulation, castration complex, etc. We opted for an unconscious of superimposed, multiple strata of subjectifications, heterogeneous strata of development with greater and lesser consistency. An unconscious, thus, that is more 'schizo', liberated from familialist yokes, and turned more towards current praxis than towards fixations and regressions on the past. An unconscious of flux and abstract machines, more than an unconscious of structure and language. (Guattari 1996b: 197–8)

The analytic problematic shifts from a backward-looking interpretation of the symptoms of pre-existing latent material to the forward-looking, pragmatic application of singularities towards the construction of new universes of reference for subjectification. The heavy reliance on the castration complex that marked Guattari's early writings was subject, by the time of *Anti-Oedipus*, to a definitive critique; which is also to say that it didn't definitively go away.[4] Rather, over the years since that time Guattari's emphasis changed so much that it is deployed as a point of contrast.

With these points in mind let's consider what remains of transversality. I am not so much interested in its diverse adjectival deployments. Rather, it seems to me that stripped of its overt psychoanalytic scaffolding (except for the modified theory of partial objects) and the institutional analytic framework in which it was originally conceived and practised for some 30 years, the concept is radically opened to hitherto unimagined mutations and complexifications across all sorts of domains. In other words, transversality still signifies militant, social, undisciplined creativity. Guattari was well aware of the risks of this kind of openness and of the concept's progressive deterritorialization from existing modelizations. He emphasized that transversality was not a given, an 'already there', but always to be conquered through a pragmatics of existence' (Guattari 1995a: 125). In his early works transversality needed to be released and consolidated through some specific institutional activity, but not towards a norm given in advance. Transversality was an adjustable, *real* coefficient, decentred and non-hierarachical, and *Chaosmosis* put the accent on its in-betweenness. Transversality as a 'bridge' (i.e. across strata in an ontological dimension, or in relation to one or more dimensions) is an idea that occurs several times; the concept retained its break with horizontal and vertical coordinates, its deterritorializing character, its social and political experimentality, and connection with production, especially the production of subjectivity, and the collective assemblages of enunciation. Transversality remained a line rather than a point. A line that picks up speed in the middle as it travels between relatively autonomous components of subjectification. Transversality can accelerate in the middle, but it better watch out for the 'speed[s] of subjugation' (Deleuze and Guattari, 1984: 349): the swiftness of reactionary clampdowns and liquidations, and any professional recourse to ready-made categories, conservative reterritorializations and diversionary phantasms.

Guattari's emphasis on analytic methods to modify introjected objects places the emphasis on mental ecology and the 'object' in question in the later work is ecosophic. Ecology is vital to the consideration of how to model the psyche in a way that is sensitive to a world tied up in impasses of every kind. We know that the old topographies of the psyche have been abandoned by Guattari. In Guattari's (1995a: 91) hands, 'an ecology of the virtual is . . . just as pressing as ecologies of the visible world'. What he is suggesting is that Universes, one of four ontological domains alongside Fluxes, Phylums and Territories, whose domain is that of virtuality and incorporeality, that is of 'potential space', need to be understood ecologically; which is to say in terms of interrelations, interfaces, autonomous becomings. Simply put, these new, incorporeal, divergent Universes that don't realize predetermined or preexistent wholes or principles, but are genuine becomings of subjectivity, are of immense interest for Guattari: 'beyond the relations of actualized forces, virtual ecology will not simply attempt to preserve the endangered species of cultural life but equally to engender conditions for the creation and development of unprecedented formations of subjectivity that have never been seen and never felt' (1995a: 91). Guattari escapes the poverty and sterility of the simple realization-of-the-possible model by appealing to a virtual ecology in which the finite, existential Territories actualized and made visible by new media technologies (one of his examples is computer-aided design), for instance, open onto new, unprecedented incorporeal Universes in which subjectivity finds its autonomy by (re) singularizing itself. The relation between the domains moves from a real manifestation (finite Territories) to boundless virtual Universes; but the values of the latter are supported by the former. Such Universes are, Guattari (1995a: 94) notes, 'incorporeal ecosystem(s)' which he likens to the objects typical of the history of psychoanalysis, despite the latter's poverty, as a point of contrast, but also to underline especially with reference to Lacan's *objet a* – partially deterritorialized and resistant to specularization – the difficulty if not the impossibility of representing them. One hears echoes in Guattari's description of being 'transported into a Debussyist Universe' a much earlier idea of transference that he borrowed from his colleague Jacques Schotte: transference as a kind of amorous transport beyond everyday existential Territories.

Before we are ourselves amorously transported into the Universe of Guattarian theory, it is pragmatic to consider how this version of ecosophy would have sounded on the hustings as he sought office in the Paris regional elections under the banner of a Green politics that saw him move transversally between two parties: Les Verts and Génération Ecologie.

Universes lack extrinsic coordinates and are thus not open to 'direct objective representation' (Guattari, 1995a: 125). This is an important principle for Guattari because it allows him to escape a reifying scientistic superego, as it were, that plagues the analysis of mental objects. But what sort of 'objects' are these? Guattari wants to go further, to really deterritorialize them and get outside his own fourfold domains so as to posit a 'pre-objectal entity' transversal to all the domains, not subject to space and time, speech, representation, and only whose slowing down from its alleged 'infinite velocity' enables the existence of more properly speaking 'objects' which subjectivity uses to forge itself to be deduced. This peculiar 'being before being' is Guattari's (1995a: 126) attempt to finally elude pre-established coordinates by borrowing the idea of the pre-verbal, emergent subjectivity of the potential space between the paradoxically undivided and sharable yet soon to be divided affective space between self and (m)other (Guattari, 1996b: 195); elsewhere, he calls it the 'included middle' (see page 36). With this 'pre-objectal' and 'pre-personal' logic, irreducible to the individual and dichotomaniac closures, Guattari posits here the existence of a primary, instinctual subjectivity on the model of the primary process postulated by Freud; indeed, the same language is used by Guattari to describe the catalysing of fragments of Fluxes in finite existential

Territories – in Freud the 'binding' of impulses – and their embodiment in the unspoken name of Eros over Thanatos (Guattari [see pages 35–6] does, here and there, nod to Thanatos as one possibility in the 'praxic opening' of existential Territories). Despite his rigorous rewriting, and the originality of his own theoretical metapsychology, Guattari's model remains, despite himself, the Freudian Unconscious, further deterritorialized (just think of Guattari's criteria listed above and strongly recall Freud's characterizations of the Unconscious: included middle or exemption from contradiction, mobility, timelessness, replacement of extrinsic coordinates). The question remains: which Freud did Guattari retain?

Conclusion

If Freud's dualistic metapsychology ultimately comes down on the side of death, of the death drive over Eros, then Guattari's concept of transversality and his theory of the group subject are radically anti-Freudian at least as far as metapsychology is concerned. To put it another way, Guattari stakes a sociological claim with Eros, while Freud chooses an anti-sociological principle in the name of Thanatos. For Guattari, Eros and the group triumph over Thanatos and the individual. All of Guattari's psychoanalytic debts are paid off with this decision: he resists Freud by enforcing Eros and society over the death drive of the narcissistic individual. The narcissist is coerced into sociality in the name of the creative spirit and sexual instinct, of the myth that love is not in the end conquered by death. Guattari is anti-Freudian and anti-Lacanian, but thoroughly psychoanalytic (see Dufresne 2000).

Transversality rests, then, on group Eros. Nothing and no one is brought into communication without it. Indeed, if Guattari's goal is the modification of the introjects of the superego, the establishment of a 'new group law', then his conception of the superego demands that it is not irreparably tainted by the death drive. Now, in the service of Eros, Guattari does not demand of the group that it definitively exorcise the death phantasies of individuals. Rather, individuals may re-experience such phantasies in the group, but group identity will check the retreat of their death instincts into narcissistic solitude by providing a setting and experimental routines in which they may be actualized and even maintained (Eros is, after all, a great preserver). The Eros of the group makes, as Guattari notes, certain demands on individuals, one of which is the assailability of individual phantasies; the group may even demand that the individual abandon the phantasy of group belonging. Guattari not only resists the Freudian death drive, but the legacy of the dualistic metapsychology. He does this by developing a conception of the individual as fundamentally a group, a social subject, a group subject, of which there are two kinds. The choice of Eros entails the group subject, that is, a definition beyond the traditional dualities of society and individual, Eros and Thanatos. Guattari was well aware that his early conceptualization of the superego and the social were, for example, too dualistic; in his later work he sought to overcome the heavy philosophical burdens of threes with models composed of four dimensions, connected transversally, but still, in a fairly obvious way, aligned with Freudian concepts: Fluxes (unconscious) – Phylums (drives) – Universes (complexes) – Territories (transference). In those cases where he retains some kind of triad, as in *The Three Ecologies*, he dearly states that he is not 'going beyond' Freudianism but reassessing and reorienting it towards the future.

Ultimately, transversality may be best appreciated in terms of its praxic opening and the virtual potential it holds for subjectification. While the gamble of Eros risks the misunderstanding of a myth of group togetherness, Guattari did not fail to point out that transversality was only livable according to diverse modalities involving as much crisis and banality as responsibility for innovation and the challenge of its permanent reappraisal.

I am greatly indebted to the astute comments of my colleague Todd Dufresne, Department of Philosophy, Lakehead University. I would also like to thank Mike Gane for specific suggestions regarding an earlier version of this paper which I presented at the Graduate Programme in Social and Political Thought at York University, Toronto, Ontario.

Notes

Translators' Introduction

1 For the concept of the body without organs, see note 68 of *The Three Ecologies*.

2 All quotations from 'When the Earth Screamed' are taken from the first one-volume edition of *The Professor Challenger Stories*.

3 For an overview of the possibility of human extinction, see John Leslie's *The End of the World: The Science and Ethics of Human Extinction*, which covers the destruction of the ozone layer, pollution, drug-resistant diseases, nuclear war, and biological and chemical warfare; as well as 'natural disasters' such as asteroids, comets and supernovae; 'man-made disasters' such as genetic engineering or high-energy experiments in physics; and finally 'risks from philosophy': not only religious fundamentalism, but ethical relativism and even Schopenhauerian pessimism. Indeed, as Leslie remarks, 'it could seem surprising that the human race has survived so long'.

4 See Friedrich Nietzsche's remarks on the eternal return in *The Will to Power*, sections 1065 and 1067.

5 A. Atiq Rahman in his excellent essay 'Climate Change and Violent Conflicts', in *Ecology, Politics and Violent Conflict* (Suliman, 1999: 183–4).

6 For a fuller discussion of Integrated World Capitalism, see Gary Genosko's Introduction to *The Guattari Reader* (Guattari, 1996b: 24–30).

7 Toby Litt's short story 'It Could Have Been Me and It Was' is a comic illustration of this, in which a man wins the Lottery and decides to believe everything the advertisements tell him:

> One Friday evening I sat down to watch *Eurotrash* and the next day I had to go out and buy a Fiat *Punto*, two Renault *Clios*, a

Volkswagen *Polo*, a Citröen *Xantia*, some *Monster Munch*, *Crunchy Nut Cornflakes*, a Cadbury's *Twirl* and a packet of Wrigley's *Spearmint Gum*, Andrews *Antacid Indigestion Tablets* (which came in quite handy after I'd eaten the Monster Munch), Colgate *Bicarbonate of Soda Toothpaste* (which overcame the ill-effects of the chewing gum), a large box of Tampax tampons and a pack of *Energizer* batteries. (Litt, 1997: 4–5)

8   Estimated population figures from the British Trust for Ornithology.

9   This is only to be expected when, in Britain for example, 92 per cent of people watch television for more than an hour a day (see Chapman *et al.*, 1997: 222).

10   Proust, 1996: 252–3, italics added. See also note 25 of *The Three Ecologies*.

11   Cited in Prigogine and Stengers, 1985: 73, italics added.

12   As Deleuze writes in *The Logic of Sense*:

Far from being individual or personal, singularities preside over the genesis of individuals and persons; they are distributed in a 'potential' which admits neither Self nor I, but which produces them by actualizing or realizing itself, although the figures of this actualization do not at all resemble the realized potential. Only a theory of singular points is capable of transcending the synthesis of the person and the analysis of the individual as these are (or are made) in consciousness. (1990: 102–3)

13   Benn, 1976: 200. Guattari and Deleuze appropriate *Lenz* to their own ends in *Anti-Oedipus*.

14   See Deleuze's 'Coldness and Cruelty' (Deleuze and Sacher-Masoch, 1989) and his return to the subject in *Essays Critical and Clinical* (1997: 53–5). In *The Three Ecologies* Guattari remarks upon the Nobel Prize-winning physicist Ilya Prigogine's belief that a 'narrative element' is essential in science. More recently, the distinguished chemist Carl Djerassi, who first synthesized the birth control pill, has turned to writing plays and novels (which he calls 'science-in-fiction') in order to liberate himself from scientific paradigms.

15   Sylvester, 1987: 54. See also Deleuze, 1981.

16   Sylvester, 1987: 140.

17   Something of the sort occurred in the financial district of London on 18 June 1999, when thousands of demonstrators – environmentalists, anarchists, anticapitalists and others – took part in a 'Carnival Against Capitalism' in protest against Third World debt, the arms trade and all the evils of IWC. It was a carefully planned day of anarchy that took the authorities completely by surprise and was co-ordinated through the Internet by hundreds of disparate protest groups. As was observed at the time, 'the very beauty of the operation was the apparent lack of organizers, leaders or any public face' (*Observer*, 20 June 1999: 'Virtual chaos baffles police: recruited through an obscure website, organized in cells, the ecowarriors without a chief have redefined anarchy'). Some comments from demonstrators: 'The way it works is that different cells work on different things . . . loads of different groups did their own thing . . . no one is in charge . . . each cell didn't know exactly what the others were doing.' The use of the Internet made the protest truly international in over 43 countries on the same day. As the J18 website declared at the time: 'Resistance will be as transnational as capital.' Other comments on the J18 website (http://www.greennet.org.uk/june18/home.html) are directly relevant to the thesis of *The Three Ecologies*:

> the global capitalist system is at the root of our social and ecological troubles . . . a system based on the 'survival of the fittest' and 'growth' can only continue to cause human misery while destroying the ecology of the planet. A new world is possible. A global movement of resistance is rising – people are reclaiming control of their lives . . . June 18th will only work if diverse movements and groups get involved: environmental, workers', women's, unwaged/unemployed, students, trade unionists, peace, pensioners, gay, anti-deportation.

18 See note 69 to *The Three Ecologies*.

19 This tendency is well documented in *Environmentalism and the Mass Media*. The authors find that mass media and communications technology is in danger of locking Northern countries into 'a ghetto of environmental self-deception', thereby helping to perpetuate poverty in the South. They observe that television in particular turns the environment into an abstract concept so that ecological issues are 'categorised within people's minds as outside their everyday experience and thus well beyond their sphere of influence in terms of bringing about change' (Chapman *et al.*, 1997: 183).

20 Our Solar System has about another five billion years left before the Sun dies, engulfing the inner planets and vaporizing any life that still exists on

Earth. For a discussion of the collapse of the universe and the 'big crunch'
see Rees, 1997: 203–20.

The Three Ecologies

1 The epigraph is taken from a paper in Gregory Bateson's *Steps to an
   Ecology of Mind* entitled 'Pathologies of Epistemology', which in itself is a
   perfect illustration of ecosophical thought. Bateson is outlining some of the
   'epistemological fallacies' of Western civilization. Whereas Charles Darwin's
   theory of natural selection argued that 'the unit of survival was either the
   family line or the species or subspecies', Bateson argues that 'the unit of
   survival is organism plus environment. We are learning by bitter experience
   that the organism which destroys its environment destroys itself.' He
   concludes that 'the unit of evolutionary survival turns out to be identical with
   the unit of mind. Formerly we thought of a hierarchy of taxa – individual,
   family line, subspecies, species, etc. – as units of survival. We now see a
   different hierarchy of units – gene-in-organism, organism-in-environment,
   ecosystem, etc. Ecology, in the widest sense, turns out to be the study
   of the interaction and survival of ideas and programs (i.e., differences,
   complexes of differences, etc.) in circuits.' The full paragraph from which
   Guattari quotes reads:

   > Let us now consider what happens when you make the
   > epistemological error of choosing the wrong unit: you end up with the
   > species versus the other species around it or versus the environment
   > in which it operates. Man against nature. You end up, in fact, with
   > Kaneohe Bay polluted. Lake Erie a slimy green mess, and 'Let's build
   > bigger atom bombs to kill off the next-door neighbours.' *There is
   > an ecology of bad ideas, just as there is an ecology of weeds*, and
   > it is characteristic of the system that basic error propagates itself. It
   > branches out like a rooted parasite through the tissues of life, and
   > everything gets into a rather peculiar mess. When you narrow down
   > your epistemology and act on the premise 'What interests me is me,
   > or my organization, or my species', you chop off consideration of other
   > loops of the loop structure. You decide that you want to get rid of the
   > by-products of human life and that Lake Erie will be a good place to
   > put them. You forget that the eco-mental system called Lake Erie is a
   > part of your wider ecomental system – and that if Lake Erie is driven
   > insane, its insanity is incorporated in the larger system of your thought
   > and experience. (1972: 484)

The point being that, as Guattari says, 'nature cannot be separated from culture; in order to comprehend the interactions between eco-systems, the mechanosphere and the social and individual Universes of reference, we must learn to think "transversally"' (see p. 29). There is an interesting résumé of Bateson's restless career in *Anti-Oedipus* (1984: 236). [Tr.]

2   For a wider discussion of ecosophy see 'The Ecosophic Object' in *Chaosmosis*. While it shares with traditional ecology a concern for biological species and the biosphere, ecosophy also recognizes 'incorporeal species' that are equally endangered, and an entire 'mental ecology' in crisis: 'How do we change mentalities, how do we reinvent social practices that would give back to humanity – if it ever had it – a sense of responsibility, not only for its own survival, but equally for the future of all life on the planet, for animal and vegetable species, likewise for incorporeal species such as music, the arts, cinema, the relation with time, love and compassion for others, the feeling of fusion at the heart of the Cosmos?' [Tr.]

3   At Fiat factories, for example, the salaried manpower has decreased from 140,000 workers to 60,000 in a dozen years, while productivity has increased by 75 per cent. [Trans.: Guattari is not advocating a more passive, consumerist 'leisure time': 'Certainly, machinism tends to liberate more and more "freetime". But free for what? To devote oneself to prefabricated leisure activities? To stay glued to the television?' (Guattari, 1996b: 270).]

4   Guattari clarifies this point in *Chaosmosis*: 'Large movements of subjectification don't necessarily develop in the direction of emancipation. The massive subjective revolution which has been developing among the Iranian people for more than ten years is focused on religious archaisms and generally conservative attitudes – particularly with regard to the position of women' (1995a: 2). [Tr.]

5   On 26 April 1986, an explosion occurred in Reactor 4 at the Chernobyl power station in the Ukraine. The radioactive cloud of the blast spread over much of Europe, contaminating flora and fauna. Left to itself, the reactor should have shut itself down automatically, but operators accidentally overrode the safety systems. There is currently an 18-mile exclusion zone around the power station and there are fears that the concrete casing that covers Reactor 4 is inadequate to prevent further leakages and blasts ten times worse than the last. If this occurs, the only methods left to contain the disaster will be sand bombing and mass evacuation. The Tokaimura nuclear accident in Japan on 30 September 1999 was the world's most serious since Chernobyl. Again, it was a classic case of human error, when workers made a simple mistake preparing liquid uranium for use in a reactor. [Tr.]

6 See *Anti-Oedipus* (1984: 79–84, 360) and *A Thousand Plateaus* (1988: 40), where the 'double pincer' is related to Gregory Bateson's 'double bind', a term coined by Bateson to characterize the no-win situation faced by a person who is receiving contradictory messages from another, more powerful person. He believed it may be a root cause of schizophrenia. In *Anti-Oedipus*, however, Guattari and Deleuze look at the example of the father–son relationship and regard the 'double bind' as oedipalizing rather than schizophrenizing. For Bateson's definition of the term see *Steps to an Ecology of Mind* (1972: 206–27). [Tr.]

7 Although the Cold War was not formally ended until 1990, this is Guattari's post-Cold War response to his previous alignment of the class struggle with East–West relations. See for example *Communists Like Us*:

> It's only too evident that every effort at taking control of the length of the work day, by the movement of the new subjectivities, will be illusory if it does not attack frontally the network of command put in place by Integrated World Capitalism. To tackle this network means putting in question the East–West relation, to derail the mechanism integrating the two superpowers, which has overcoded, from the 1970s until today [1985], all international relations. Breaking the relation of domination laboriously established between capitalism and socialism, and radically reversing the alliances . . . in the direction of the North–South axis, against the East–West axis, constitutes an essential foundation for recomposing the intellectual and working-class proletariat in the advanced capitalist countries. (Guattari and Negri, 1990: 134–5) [Tr.]

8 It is Guattari's contention that Integrated World Capitalism has successfully 'neutralized' the working classes, offering them a 'pseudo-participation' in political debate as 'consumers'. This 'ever more marked integration of the more privileged sections of the working class into the ideology, lifestyle and interests of the middle classes' has resulted in 'the decay of working-class political life'. The working classes have entered 'a period of generalized subjugation by means of the mass media' (1984: 196, 249–50, 264, translation modified). [Tr.]

9 Generally, introjection is the process by which the external world is incorporated into an individual's psyche. Freud suggested that the subject/object, or ego/outside world opposition, results from the introjection of that which is perceived as pleasurable and the projection of anything deemed unpleasurable. Closely linked to orality, introjection may be conceived of in terms of ingestion (eating) and projection in terms of rejection (spitting out). The role of pleasure is important here, as it relates to the seductiveness of consumerism, the media, etc. It is the process by which, as Guattari states later, IWC infiltrates the most unconscious subjective strata. For a succinct definition of the term see Laplanche and Pontalis, 1988: 229–31. [Tr.]

10   'Serialism' here refers to Jean-Paul Sartre's notion of 'serial being' in *The Critique of Dialectical Reason* (Volume I, Chapter 4) which Guattari summarizes in an article in *Chimères*: 'The members of a series are united in being turned towards an exterior object, in which they have a common interest, without having a project in common and without necessarily being aware of one another. The unity of the series is not active, rather, it is passive and contingent because it is prefabricated.' For Guattari, it is important to 'move out of seriality . . . and into processes of singularization, which restore to existence what one might call its auto-essentialization' (see 1996b: 201, 203n11). [Tr.]

11   Nationalitary (*nationalitaire*) demands are not to be confused with national demands, for the latter arise from a majority, whereas the former arise from a minority that is often in conflict with the majority. See *A Thousand Plateaus*: 'the birth of nations implies many artifices: Not only are they constituted in an active struggle against the imperial or evolved systems, the feudal systems, and the autonomous cities, but they crush their own "minorities", in other words, minoritarian phenomena that could be termed "nationalitarian", which work from within and if need be turn to the old codes to find a greater degree of freedom' (Deleuze and Guattari, 1988: 456). [Tr.]

12   Manicheism is an Asiatic religion founded by Mani, a Persian born in Babylonia *c*. AD 216. In essence, Mani's religion is based on the struggle between two eternal conflicting principles, such as God/ matter, light/ darkness; hence Guattari's shorthand use of 'Manicheism' to mean any dualistic mode of thought (see 'Manichean dualism' and 'systems of Manichean bipolar valorizations' in 1995a: 111, 29). [Tr.]

13   Guattari and Deleuze make frequent use of the verb *devenir* (becoming), especially compounds such as *devenir-femme*, *devenir-enfant*, *devenir-animal*, *devenir-végétal*, *devenir-minéral*, *devenir-moléculaire*, etc. The concept is fully discussed in *A Thousand Plateaus*: 'Becoming is certainly not imitating, or identifying with something; neither is it regressing-progressing; neither is it corresponding, establishing corresponding relations; neither is it producing, producing a filiation or producing through filiation. Becoming is a verb with a consistency all its own; it

does not reduce to, or lead back to, "appearing", "being", "equalling" or "producing"' (1988: 239). It is perhaps best described as 'an absolute deterritorialization . . . a creative line of escape that says nothing other than what it is' (Deleuze and Guattari, 1986: 35–6). [Tr.]

14 In his *Capitalism and Material Life 1400–1800*, Fernand Braudel argues that material life progresses by means of 'slow evolutions'. Progress is a gradual, frequently interrupted process rather than one of rapid and uninterrupted growth. Advances occur 'very slowly over long periods by the initiative of groups of men, not individuals (the exceptions prove the rule), and in countless varied and obscure ways'. Great technical revolutions infiltrate society 'slowly and with difficulty . . . to speak of revolution here is to use a figure of speech. Nothing took place at break-neck speed' (1973: xi, 285, 442). [Tr.]

15 In Guattari's transversalist conception of subjectivity, he proposes an interface between 'existential Territories' and 'incorporeal Universes'. The former are singular, idiosyncratic, sensible and finite, the latter are non-dimensioned, non-coordinated, trans-sensible and infinite. During the process of 'chaosmic folding', the subject oscillates between the two: finite personal worlds of constraints, limits and coordinates (existential Territories), and Universes of infinite speed where all extrinsic references and coordinates disappear, with unforeseeable consequences: 'I am no longer as I was before, I am swept away by a becoming other, carried beyond my familiar existential Territories' (1995a: 93). [Tr.]

16 The concept of 'praxis' (from the Greek for 'doing') originated in Karl Marx's early writings. It suggests action rather than philosophical speculation, and for Guattari it means 'effective practices of experimentation' (see p. 22). [Tr.]

17 Generally the term *dispositif* refers to the manner in which the pieces or organs of an apparatus or device are arranged, or to the mechanism itself. It is often translated as 'set-up' or representational 'apparatus'. However, it has appeared in other translations as 'assemblage'. To add to the terminological confusion, *agencement*, normally translated as 'assemblage' (see note 30), has been sometimes translated as 'set-up' or even 'layout'. Here we have chosen to invent an English word by way of a solution. [Tr.]

18 In everyday French *mot d'ordre* means 'slogan', but in the work of Guattari and Deleuze it designates an imperative function immanent to language, an 'order-word'. In *A Thousand Plateaus* they argue that 'language is made not to be believed but to be obeyed, and to compel obedience'. State functionaries (politicians, the police, teachers, etc.) represent 'an abominable faculty consisting in emitting, receiving, and transmitting order-words'; they 'tell us what we "must" think'. This is why the order-word is defined as 'the elementary unit of language . . . very short phrases that command life and are inseparable from enterprises and large-scale projects'. The Nazis understood the insidious, transformative power of order-words, as did the Marxists when they invented the slogan 'Workers of the World, Unite!', thereby extracting from the masses a nascent proletarian class. The danger for any ecosophical movement with agreed aims and objectives is that it could produce oppressive and reductive order-words of a similar potency that would prohibit the emergence of new collective subjectivities and would encourage the election of a media-friendly leader (the sound-bite). Guattari is advocating a union of processes of singularity, a collective intentionality, a 'being-for', rather than a 'being-against' which only relies on 'impotent catchphrases of resentment' [1996b: 252]. For a full exploration of the function of the order-word see *A Thousand Plateaus* (Deleuze and Guattari, 1988: 75–89, 106–10). [Tr.]

19 Phallocentrism is, as the name suggests, a mode of thought that privileges the phallus, or rather, male attitudes to the world and to women. The term was first coined by the psychoanalyst Ernest Jones (1879–1958) who criticized classical psychoanalysis for its overemphasis on the penis and phallic symbolism, particularly the tendency to view the psychological development of the female as a reaction to the discovery that she 'lacks' a penis. Although they have not escaped charges of sexism themselves (especially Guattari's concept of 'becoming-woman', see note 50), Guattari and Deleuze advocate a defiantly nonsymbolic, functionalist approach to organs of any kind, even the sexual organs, be they male or female (see 1988: 256). [Tr.]

20 Telematics is described in the *OED* as '(the science of) the long-distance transmission of computer information. So *telematic* – of or pertaining to telematics'. [Tr.]

21 Guattari is of course referring to the famous Cartesian formula *cogito, ergo sum*: 'I am thinking, therefore I exist.' For a discussion of the role of the *cogito* (as the formula is often called) in processes of subjectification see *A Thousand Plateaus* (1988: 130–2); Guattari and Deleuze return to the *cogito* as an example of a signed philosophical concept in their last book together, *What is Philosophy?* (1994: 24–27). [Tr.]

22 In *A Thousand Plateaus* Guattari and Deleuze emphasize the 'necessarily social character of enunciation'. There are no individual statements, only collective assemblages of enunciation: 'Every statement is the product of a machinic assemblage, in other words, of collective agents of enunciation (take "collective agents" to mean not peoples or societies but multiplicities).' If there is no individual enunciation, it follows that 'there is not even a subject of enunciation . . . the statement is individuated, and enunciation subjectified, only to the extent that an impersonal collective assemblage requires it and determines it to be so . . . a subject is never the condition of possibility of language or the cause of the statement: there is no subject, only collective assemblages of enunciation. Subjectification is simply one such assemblage and designates a formalization of expression or a regime of signs rather than a condition internal to language' (1988: 37, 79–80, 130). [Tr.]

23 Guattari's use of the feminine noun *saisie* is meant to evoke no doubt, the additional notion of data capture, *la saisie de données*. Guattari's use of two terms usually associated with the cinema: *cadrer* and *mise en scène*, suggest that here the *dis-positional* might be thought of in relation to the *hors-champ* or off-screen, as the field constitutive of the cinematic frame. Guattari appears to be speaking here of the *hors-champs* as that which determines (sets the boundaries for) the existence and intelligibility of discourse, cinematic or otherwise. For a consideration of Guattari's thoughts on the cinema, see 'Le Cinéma: Un Art Mineur' in *La révolution moléculaire* (1977: 201–38). [Tr.]

24 According to Blaise Pascal (1623–62) there are two sorts of mind: the mathematical mind (*esprit de géométrie*) and the intuitive mind (*esprit de finesse*). He argues that it is rare for mathematicians to be intuitive, because they 'cannot see what is in front of them' and want to 'begin with definitions, followed by principles'. Intuitive people, on the other hand, are not mathematical, but can 'judge at a single glance' and 'feel' what cannot be demonstrated logically (Pascal, 1995: 150–1). [Tr.]

25 In Guattari's writings the French word *ritournelle* has been variously translated as 'ritornello' or 'refrain'. We have chosen the latter, in line with the translator of *A Thousand Plateaus*, the eleventh plateau of which, 'Of the Refrain', deals with the concept in detail (1988: 310–50). In 'Ritournelles et Affects existentiels' in *Cartographies schizoanalytiques* Guattari usefully summarizes the concept of the refrain:

> Under the generic term of refrain, I would place reiterative discursive sequences that are closed in upon themselves and whose function

is an extrinsic catalysing of existential affects. Refrains can find substance in rhythmic and plastic forms, in prosodic segments, in facial traits, in the emblems of recognition, in leitmotifs, signatures, proper names or their invocational equivalents; they can just as well be found transversally between different substances – this is the case with Proust's 'refrains of lost time', which are constantly entering into correspondence with each other. They can just as well be of a sensory order (the madeleine dipped in the cup of tea, the uneven paving stones in the courtyard of the Guermantes's Hotel, the 'little phrase' of Vinteuil, the plastic compositions around the bell tower of Martinville) as of a problematic order (the ambience in the salon of the Verdurins), as of a facial order (Odette's face). (1989a: 257; and 1996b: 162)

For a fuller account of Proustian refrains see the final section of *L'inconscient machinique*, 'Les Ritoumelles du Temps Perdu' (1979: 237–336), in which Guattari quotes the following from *In Search of Lost Time* regarding the existentializing refrain of the 'little phrase' of the andante of Vinteuil's sonata, which Swann associates with his love for Odette: 'But the little phrase, as soon as it struck his ear, had the power to liberate in him the space that was needed to contain it; the proportions of Swann's soul were altered; a margin was left for an enjoyment [*jouissance*] that corresponded no more than his love for Odette to any external object and yet was not, like his enjoyment of that love, purely individual, but assumed for him a sort of reality superior to that of concrete things' (Proust, 1996: 284–5). [Tr.]

26 A stroboscope is any device that presents a series of still pictures in rapid succession, such as a film projector. Guattari is alluding to the phenomenon of stroboscopic movement (or apparent movement), when we perceive continuous movement in response to a rapid succession of static views. The philosopher Henri Bergson (1859–1941) was one of the first to make a connection between stroboscopic movement and our perception of the world, concluding that 'the mechanism of our ordinary knowledge is of a cinematographical kind' (1928: 323). For an extended analysis of cinematographic perception after Bergson see Deleuze's *Cinema 1: The Movement-Image* (1986) and *Cinema 2: The Time-Image* (1989). [Tr.]

27 In *Anti-Oedipus* Guattari and Deleuze criticize Freud's use of Greek theatre as a model of subjectification. The Oedipus complex is an attempt to restore order to the unconscious, 'an order made classical owing to the

ancient Greek theatre . . . The unconscious ceases to be what it is – a
factory, a workshop – to become a theatre, a scene and its staging
. . . The psychoanalyst becomes a director for a private theatre, rather
than an engineer or mechanic' (1984: 54–5). The powerful model of
subjectification that is the courtly love tradition, with all its attendant ideals
and attitudes – what one might call a 'courtship assemblage' (Deleuze
and Guattari, 1988: 324) – continues to influence heterosexual relations
to this day. Its inspiration is feudal, a variation on the theme of vassalage
to an overlord, but also religious, drawing on a tradition of devotion to
the Virgin Mary. The lover of the early romances idealizes his beloved and
longs for union with her in order to attain moral perfection. As Deleuze
remarks, 'the feudal machine combines new relationships with the earth,
war, the animal, but also with culture and games (tournaments), with
woman (courtly love): all sorts of fluxes enter into conjunction' (Deleuze
and Parnet, 1987: 70; see also 74–5). Guattari and Deleuze are fond of
the twelfth-century writer Chrétien de Troyes, author of the earliest extant
Arthurian courtly romance, the unfinished *Conte du graal* (or *Perceval*):
'Open Chrétien de Troyes to any page and you will find a catatonic knight
seated on his steed, leaning on his lance, waiting, seeing the face of
his loved one in the landscape; you have to hit him hard to make him
respond' (Deleuze and Guattari, 1988: 174). [Tr.]

28   For a useful discussion of the distinctions between 'phantasy' and
'fantasy' see Laplanche and Pontalis's *The Language of Psychoanalysis*:

> The German word *Phantasie* means imagination, though less in the
> philosophical sense of the faculty of imagining (*Einbildungskraft*) than in
> the sense of the world of the imagination, its contents and the creative
> activity which animates it. Freud exploited these different connotations
> of the common German usage. In French, the term *fantasme* was
> revived by psychoanalysis, with the result that it has more philosophical
> overtones than its German equivalent; nor does it correspond exactly
> to the German, in that it has a more restricted extension: *fantasme*
> refers to a specific imaginary production, not to the world of phantasy
> and imaginative activity in general.

They note that most English psychoanalysts use the term 'phantasy',
while Americans have tended to use 'fantasy' (1988: 314–19). [Tr.].

29   Guattari is no doubt referring here to the work of Jacques Lacan whose
project involved the revision of Freudian psychoanalytic theory through the
prism of structural linguistics. He stated famously that 'the unconscious
is structured like a language' (1987: 20), emphasizing that 'every analytic

phenomenon, every phenomenon that comes from the analytic field, from the analytic discovery, from what we are dealing with in symptoms and neurosis, is structured like a language' (*The Seminar. Book III. The Psychoses*, 167). Lacan maintained a distinction between linguistics and what he called *la linguisterie* (possibly a conflation of *linguistique* and *connerie*, given Lacan's association of *linguisterie* with *la bêtise* – stupidity). The former represented the 'science' so to speak, of language, the latter the unformalized dimensions of language, the language of the unconscious revealed when language begins to break down. For a useful introduction to the work of Lacan and for a discussion of some of these ideas, see Benvenuto and Kennedy, *The Works of Jacques Lacan: An Introduction* (1986). Guattari has criticized Lacan's return to Freud, suggesting that 'he read Freud entirely in bad faith' (Stivale, 1985: 10). He argues that Lacan's extrapolation of the signifier from Freud is 'un-Freudian': 'There is a Freudian creativity that is much closer to theatre, to myth, to the dream, and which has little to do with this structuralist, systemic, mathematizing . . . thought of Lacan' (Stivale, 1985: 10–11). For a useful summary of Guattari and Deleuze's objections to Lacanian psychoanalysis see 'Dead Psychoanalysis: Analyse' in Deleuze and Parnet's *Dialogues*. [Tr.].

30 We have followed earlier translations in rendering *agencement* as 'assemblage'. It is important, however, to bear in mind the fact that the French word is both a noun and a verb, an 'arrangement' and the act of 'arranging'. [Tr.]

31 In English in the original. Perhaps a reference to James Joyce's *Finnegans Wake*, which was originally known as *Work in Progress* until Joyce finally revealed the title. See, for example, *Our Exagmination Round His Factification for Incamination of Work in Progress* by Samuel Beckett *et al*. Guattari and Deleuze borrow the word 'chaosmos' from *Finnegans Wake* (see Joyce, 1960: 118; Deleuze, 1990: 176; Deleuze, 1994: 57, 69, 121; and, of course, Guattari's *Chaosmosis* [1995a]). [Tr.]

32 More accurately, in *The Trial* Titorelli does paint different judges but they all want to be depicted with the same authority and gravitas: 'this was obviously the portrait of a Judge. Also it strikingly resembled the portrait hanging in the Advocate's office. True, this was quite a different Judge . . . Yet everything else showed a close resemblance' (Kafka, 1987: 161). See the discussion surrounding the 'proliferation of photos and portraits in *The Trial* from Fräulein Bürstner's room to Titorelli's studio' in *Kafka: Toward a Minor Literature*: 'In *The Trial* we see a proliferating power of the photo, of the portrait, of the image . . . From the photos of Fräulein Bürstner we move to the obscene images in the judge's book, then to the photos of Elsa that K. shows to Leni . . . then to the unlimited series of Titorelli's tableaux, about which one could say, à la Borges, that they contain so many differences from each other because they are absolutely identical' (Deleuze and Guattari, 1986: 61). [Tr.]

33 *Entre le temps et l'éternité*, Paris: Fayard, 1988. [Trans: 'The creation of a new species signifies that among [several] micro-events some have taken on meaning [*sens*] . . . The fact that any event can "take on meaning [*sens*]" ceases to be a mere noise in the nonsensical uproar of microscopic activity, and introduces into physics that narrative element which is indispensable to a true conception of evolution' (Prigogine and Stengers, 1988: 47, 61)].

34 A brief definition of micropolitics would be 'a politics of desire that questions all situations' (Guattari, 1986: 42). For a full explanation of the term see 'Towards a Micro-Politics of Desire' and 'The Micro-Politics of Fascism' in *Molecular Revolution* (Guattari, 1984: 82–107, 217–32) and *A Thousand Plateaus* (Deleuze and Guattari, 1988: 208–31): 'In short, everything is political, but every politics is simultaneously a macropolitics and a micropolitics.' [Tr.]

35 Paul Virilio is perhaps best known for his work on visual perception in relation to concepts of speed and space. He has analysed the increasingly remote control exercised by those in power and has explored the effects for contemporary culture of what he has called the 'vision machine'. The increasing 'automation of perception' (1994: 59) and the introduction of 'automatic-perception prosthes[es]' (1994: 60) has, Virilio argues, radically altered the way in which human beings perceive and interact with their environment; it has also, of course, brought into question received wisdom concerning perception itself. Significantly, Virilio has noted how the politics of speed ultimately deprives people of their natural habitats. See *Speed and Politics: An Essay on Dromology* (1986), *War and Cinema* (1989), *The Aesthetics of Disappearance* (1991) and *The Vision Machine* (1994); see also Jean Baudrillard, *The Gulf War Did Not Take Place* (1995); see also Armitage (1997, *Angelaki*: 199–209) [Tr.]

36 Alain Bombard (*b.* 1924) is a doctor, biologist and Senior Member of the European Parliament. He has dedicated his life to a study of marine biology, establishing and presiding over several marine laboratories, such as Le Coryphène and the Fondation océanographique Ricard.

In later years he has reported to various political bodies on ecological and environmental issues. His books include *Protégeons la mer* (1977), *Histoire d'un naufragé volontaire* (1979) *La Mer et l'homme* (1980) and *Sauver la vie* (1984). [Tr.]

37 Situated on the Mediterranean coast, close to the mouth of the Rhône, Marseille is France's largest port and an important industrial centre. The Mediterranean has been described as 'the most oil-polluted sea in the world' with Marseille and the Rhône delta singled out as pollution hot spots. See the Greenpeace website for further information (http://www. greenpeace.org). [Tr.]

38 Venice is situated at the Northernmost tip of the Adriatic Sea in the lagoon formed between the mouths of the Po and Piave rivers. An ageing city, it has suffered physical damage from flooding, sinkage, air and water pollution. The mutant algae to which Guattari refers has become a significant problem, particularly during the summer months, when its rapid growth chokes the lagoon. Agricultural fertilizers, washed by rain into the lagoon, are believed to be responsible for the spread of the algae. The problem is at its most severe in the marshy areas, now known as the *laguna morta* or 'dead lagoon'. Industrial effluent from Porto Marghera on the mainland has further exacerbated the problem; according to Greenpeace, pollution levels in the Venice lagoon are now among some of the worst in the world. [Tr.]

39 Donald Trump, US real estate construction and property developer (*b.* 1946). 'Donald Trump is real good-looking. A girl named Evans was with him and another lady. It was so strange, these people are so rich. They talked about buying a building yesterday for $500 million or something' (Warhol, 1989: 375–6). [Tr.]

40 The French word *autodestruction* usually means 'self-destruction', but we have retained the word 'auto-destruction' so as not to become entangled in questions of selfhood and intentionality. Guattari does not refer here to the actions of individuals, but to a blind process of proliferation (the free market of IWC) beyond the control of persons or groups. For this reason we have avoided translating the prefix 'auto-' as 'self-' elsewhere in the text. Once we have removed this personological dimension, however, 'auto-destruction' on a global scale implies much the same harmful consumption of limited resources as 'self-destruction'; as in this meditation on hunger from Alain Bombard: 'Hunger becomes starvation; it passes from an acute to a chronic state. We begin to consume our own proteins, and a process of self-destruction [*autodestruction*] begins.

We no longer think, we sleep or are drowsy for most of the time' (1979: 90). In psychoanalysis, the term 'auto-destruction' is often associated with the death instinct, or what Guattari calls an 'intra-psychic death drive'. Finally, in general French usage, *autodestruction* can mean 'self-abuse' or masturbation. As D. H. Lawrence observes, masturbation is 'merely the spending away of a certain force, and no return. The body remains, in a sense, a corpse, after the act of self-abuse . . . Enclosed within the vicious circle of the self, with no vital contacts outside, the self becomes emptier and emptier, till it is almost a nullus, a nothingness' (1961: 179–80). [Tr.]

41 In his celebrated 1953 paper *Transitional Objects and Transitional Phenomena* the psychoanalyst D. W. Winnicott introduced the term 'transitional object' to describe any material object used by suckling and young children to bridge the gap between the first oral object, the mother's breast and any 'true object', i.e. an object clearly differentiated from the child's own subjectivity. The transitional object – often some kind of comfort blanket – represents a position midway between the subjective and the objective: 'It comes from without from our point of view, but not so from the point of view of the baby. Neither does it come from within; it is not a hallucination' (Winnicott, 1994: 5) [Tr.]

42 Verena Andermatt Conley suggests that Guattari's use of the 'couplet "system and structure" derives from Anthony Wilden's attempt to reconcile [Jacques] Lacan and [Gregory] Bateson' (1997: 102). In his essay 'Lacan and the Discourse of the Other', Wilden argues that:

> What seems now a particularly fruitful future enterprise is to seek to read Lacan (in part) in the terms of Anglo-Saxon communicationally oriented psychotherapy and at the same time see how many of Lacan's theses extend and amplify the theoretical work of people like R. D. Laing and Gregory Bateson in England and in the United States. The phenomenological and existential basis of many of these theorists, coupled with their interest in schizophrenia as a disease of communication, has led them to employ models derived from cybernetics and general systems theory to explain communicational contexts in the terms of *loci* and relationships. The notion of *feedback* (essentially what lies behind the notions of dialectic and transference), the 'black box' concept of the subject (viewed as a locus of input and output), and Carnap's theory of object language and metalanguage provide an independent clarification of much of what Lacan is saying in his own terms. From their stated basis that all behaviour

is communication, the communications theorists may be readily interpreted in the light of the Lacanian categories of the signifier, and the Symbolic, the Imaginary and the Real. (1991: 309) [Tr.]

43 The term hypercathexis (*surinvestissement*) refers to an additional cathectic charge that supplements an already cathected perception or idea. Thus Laplanche and Pontalis suggest that 'an unconscious idea is hypercathected when a supplementary charge of instinctual energy is directed on to it'. They also note that Freud refers to hypercathexis in the context of schizophrenia, 'in the case of narcissistic withdrawal of libido onto the ego'. In addition the term describes 'the preparation for danger which permits the subject to avoid or to check the trauma: "In the case of quite a number of traumas, the difference between systems that are unprepared and systems that are well prepared through being hypercathected may be a decisive factor in determining the outcome"' (1988: 191–2). [Tr.]

44 A reference to Aristotle's four 'causes', which were rediscovered by medieval scholasticism. Aristotle argues that a full explanation of anything should say what it is made of (material cause), what it essentially is (formal cause), what brought it into being (efficient cause), and what its function or purpose is (final cause). [Tr.]

45 See note 9 above on introjection. Guattari and Deleuze have always been fascinated (and horrified) by the 'introjection of repressive power by the oppressed'. In *Anti-Oedipus* it is regarded as 'the fundamental problem of political philosophy . . . why do people still tolerate being humiliated and enslaved, to such a point, indeed, that they actually want humiliation and slavery not only for others but for themselves?' (1984: 29). The Austrian-born psychoanalyst Wilhelm Reich (1897–1957) was in their view 'the first to raise the problem of the relationship between desire and the social field' and was 'the true founder of a materialist psychiatry' (1984: 118). See his *The Mass Psychology of Fascism* (1975: 53–8), which in many respects anticipates Guattari and Deleuze's concept of 'microfascism' as the only answer to their question: 'Why does desire desire its own repression?' (Deleuze and Guattari, 1988: 215); the point being that even the most leftist organizations such as trade unions and workers' movements are not immune to desiring oppression or microfascism. Desiring oppression also operates on a global scale, when 'the workers of the rich nations actively participate in the exploitation of the Third World, the arming of dictatorships, and the pollution of the atmosphere' (1988: 225). [Tr.]

46 In the Marxist theory of labour value, surplus value is the value remaining when the worker's daily costs of subsistence have been subtracted from the value of the material assets that he produces. Guattari argues that capitalism also appropriates as surplus value immaterial assets such as sensibility and desire. See *Communists Like Us* where 'life time' finds itself overcoded by 'the time of capital, or the capacity to translate every sequence of life into terms of exchange', which leads to 'an unlimited penetration of people's attitudes, sensibility and minds' (Guattari and Negri, 1990: 53). [Tr.]

47 Through the media, capitalistic subjectivity attempts to conceal from us 'a sense of finitude' (Guattari, 1996b: 272). [Tr.]

48 Célestin Freinet established the Modern School Movement in 1926. By the time of his death in 1966, it involved 10,000 schools in 33 countries. He developed three complementary teaching techniques: (1) the 'learning walk', during which pupils would join him in exploratory walks around town, gathering information and impressions about their community (a pedagogical application of the *dérive*; see note 51). Afterwards, the children would collectively dictate a collective 'free text', which might lead to 'pretexts' for direct action within their community to improve living conditions (local councils were particularly wary of Freinet's pupils); (2) a classroom printing press, for producing multiple copies of the pupils' writings and a newspaper to be distributed to their families, friends and other schools; (3) inter-school networks: pupils from two different schools exchange 'culture packages', printed texts, letters, tapes, photographs, maps, etc. Several of these twinned schools would then join to form a 'cluster', in an effort to represent as many national regions and countries as possible, leading to global learning networks especially useful for foreign-language teaching. Freinet's popular pedagogy was a response to the centralized curriculum and fixed methodologies imposed from above by the French educational authorities. He made a distinction between methodologies, which encouraged an uncritical imitation of pre-established criteria, and his own techniques, which shaped new social contexts and were 'integrated with something lived', establishing unforeseen relationships between students, teachers and parents. Methodologies are imposed from above, whereas Freinet's techniques

> ascend exclusively from the base, from our own work, and from the life of the children in our transformed classes . . . we do not present an immutable framework, nor a ceremony from which a teacher may not deviate for any reason on earth upon pain of undermining and

betraying the spirit in whose name this rigidity was imposed. Instead we offer: techniques which we have fully tested, which teachers have created in large part, perfecting and adapting them to their needs.

Literacy is motivated through issues that have a direct impact on children's lives, their families, and their communities: 'current social and economic issues, such as unemployment . . . inadequacy of local parks and playgrounds, pollution, nuclear power, children living in poverty and famine in Africa'. So many teachers in Freinet's network demanded government support for their project that teachers in France pay nothing to use the postal service for educational purposes; although new technologies such as faxes and e-mail have come to replace the printing press and the post (see Cummins and Sayers, 1995: 124–36). [Tr.]

49 Guattari defines heterogenesis as 'processes of continuous resingularization' (p. 45). It is an active, immanent singularization of subjectivity, as opposed to a transcendent, universalizing and reductionist homogenization. Heterogeneity is an expression of desire, of a becoming that is always in the process of adapting, transforming and modifying itself in relation to its environment. Whereas the State works by homogenizing (macropolitical consensus), it is always already defeated by heterogeneous formations whose singularity cannot be represented (micropolitical dissensus). However much organizations attempt to homogenize desire, something always escapes or leaks out (the 'line of flight'). There is a neat summary of this process in *A Thousand Plateaus* (1988: 218), using the Church, the Law, the Army and the State as examples. [Tr.]

50 Because the standard measure of a majority is Man, 'women, regardless of their numbers, are a minority, definable as a state or subset; but they create only by making possible a becoming over which they do not have ownership, into which they themselves must enter; this is a becoming-woman affecting all of humankind, men and women both' (Deleuze and Guattari, 1988: 106). For Guattari's views on the women's movement, see *Communists Like Us* (Guattari and Negri, 1990: 43–4) or *Anti-Oedipus*: 'The Women's Liberation movements are correct in saying: We are not castrated, so you get fucked' (1984: 61). See also Philip Goodchild's excellent summary of Guattari and Deleuze's relation to Feminism (1996: 135–39). [Tr.]

51 Guattari is surely aware of the Situationist heritage of the verb *dériver*. Inspired by Surrealist strolls, the *dérive* or drift was defined by the Situationists as the 'technique of locomotion without a goal' and it was much practised during May 1968. Guattari and Deleuze's idea of the 'schizo stroll' (Deleuze and Guattari, 1984: 2, 292) is a variation of the *dérive*, and they introduced it into the domain of theory with their concept of nomadic thought. See also Jean-François Lyotard's *Driftworks* for the notion of drifting thought. For a discussion of Guattari and Deleuze and Situationism see Sadie Plant's *The Most Radical Gesture: The Situationist International in a Postmodern Age* and Phil Baker's *Secret City*. [Tr.]

52　The root 'eco' is used here in its original Greek sense of *oïkos*, that is, 'house, domestic property, habitat, natural milieu'.

53　In psychoanalytic theory, the primary process is mental functioning operative in the id. Primary processes are conceptualized as unconscious, irrational, ignorant of time and space and governed by the pleasure–pain principle. See Freud's early formulation of the notion in his 1915 essay 'The Unconscious', in which he describes the system of the Unconscious (*Ucs.*) as consisting of instinctual or wishful impulses that are 'co-ordinate with one another' and

> exempt from mutual contradiction . . . There are in this system no negation, no doubt, no degrees of certainty . . . there are only contents, cathected with greater or lesser strength. The cathectic intensities are much more mobile [in the *Ucs.*]. By the process of *displacement* one idea may surrender to another its whole quota of cathexis; by the process of *condensation* it may appropriate the whole cathexis of several other ideas. I have proposed to regard these two processes as distinguishing marks of the so-called *primary psychical process* . . . The processes of the system *Ucs.* are *timeless*; i.e. they are not ordered temporally, are not altered by the passage of time; they have no reference to time at all . . . The *Ucs.* processes pay just as little regard to *reality*. They are subject to the pleasure principle; their fate depends only on how strong they are and on whether they fulfil the demands of the pleasure–unpleasure regulation. To sum up: *exemption from mutual contradiction*, *primary process* (mobility of cathexes), *timelessness*, and *replacement of external by psychical reality* – these are the characteristics which we may expect to find in processes belonging to the system *Ucs.* (Freud, 1984: 190–1)

See also his *New Introductory Lectures on Psychoanalysis* where the primary process is related to the id: 'The id of course knows no judgements of value: no good and evil, no morality. The economic or, if you prefer, the quantitative factor, which is intimately linked to the pleasure principle, dominates all its processes. Instinctual cathexes seeking discharge – that, in our view, is all there is in the id. It even seems that the energy of these instinctual impulses is in a state different from that in other regions of the mind, far more mobile and capable of discharge' (Freud, 1983: 107). In *Anti-Oedipus*, Guattari and Deleuze argue that Freud evaded the radical implications of his great discovery of what they call the molecular unconscious – a 'domain of free syntheses where everything is possible: endless connections, nonexclusive disjunctions, nonspecific conjunctions, partial objects and flows' – by subsequently 'discovering' the infinitely more marketable Oedipus complex, with all its attendant reassurances and redundancies, thereby inaugurating a period of analytical imperialism that persists to this day (1984: 54). [Tr.]

54 In Kleinian psychoanalysis 'good' and 'bad' objects are 'imagos which are a phantastically distorted picture of the real objects upon which they are based' (Melanie Klein, 'A Contribution to the Psychogenesis of Manic-depressive States' (1934), in *Contributions to Psycho-Analysis*, London: Hogarth, 1950). Part-objects (the penis, the breast, etc.) may be split into 'good' and 'bad' objects as a defensive mechanism against anxiety; whole objects may be similarly split, e.g. the 'bad' mother, the 'good' mother. (See Laplanche and Pontalis, 1988: 187–9 for a useful definition; see also note 9 on introjection and note 62 on part-objects.) [Tr.]

55 For an account of the phantasm and processes of subjectification see Deleuze's *The Logic of Sense*:

> What appears in the phantasm is the movement by which the ego opens itself to the surface and liberates the a-Cosmic, impersonal, and pre-individual singularities which it had imprisoned. It literally releases them like spores and bursts as it gets unburdened . . . Thus, the individuality of the ego merges with the event of the phantasm itself, even if that which the event represents in the phantasm is understood as another individual, or rather as a series of other individuals through which the dissolved ego passes. (1990: 213–14) [Tr.]

56 Here Guattari paraphrases Bateson: 'In a word, schizophrenia, deutero-learning, and the double bind cease to be matters of individual psychology and become part of the ecology of ideas in systems or "minds" whose

boundaries no longer coincide with the skins of the participant individuals'
(Bateson, 1972: 339). [Tr.]

57 See *Steps to an Ecology of Mind*:

> I speak of an action or utterance as occurring 'in' a context, and
> this conventional way of talking suggests that the particular action
> is a 'dependent' variable, while the context is the 'independent' or
> determining variable. But this view of how an action is related to its
> context is likely to distract the reader – as it has distracted me – from
> perceiving the ecology of the ideas which together constitute the small
> subsystem which I call 'context' . . . It is important to see the particular
> utterance or action as *part* of the ecological subsystem called context
> and not as the product or effect of what remains of the context after
> the piece which we want to explain has been cut out from it. (Bateson,
> 1972: 338) [Tr.]

58 Cited by Philippe Lacoue-Labarthe and Jean-Luc Nancy in *L'Absolu
littéraire: théorie de la littérature du romantisme allemand* (1978: 126).
[Trans.: Friedrich von Schlegel's famous Fragment 206 from *The
Athenaeum* is also cited by Maurice Blanchot in *The Infinite Conversation*
during a fascinating (and pertinent) discussion of Friedrich Schlegel and
the fragmentary (1993: 352–9).]

59 It is a recurrent theme in *Anti-Oedipus* that psychoanalysis oedipalizes
the neurotic, turning him or her into 'a pitiful creature who eternally
consumes daddy-and-mummy and nothing else' (1984: 20). The
neurotic is typified as someone who reduces all of their relations with
others to those of the family. Neurotics appear to have a high tolerance
for oedipalization (whereas psychotics do not). This is because neurosis
produces oedipalization itself, it is 'a desire that is already submissive and
searching to communicate its own submission' (Deleuze and Guattari,
1986: 10). Neurosis is encouraged in literature as well (whereas psychosis
is not), precisely because it is safe and comfortingly submissive. There is
an entire 'marketable neurotic conception of literature' at work (Deleuze
and Guattari, 1984: 134–5) which was comically summed up as long
ago as 1923 by an exasperated D. H. Lawrence in his essay 'Surgery for
the Novel – or a Bomb?' in which he attacks the 'lovey-dovey-darling-
take-me-to-mamma' state of literature:' "Do I love the girl or don't I?" –
"Am I pure and sweet, or am I not?" – "Do I unbutton my right glove
first, or my left?" – "Did my mother ruin my life by refusing to drink the
cocoa which my bride had boiled for her?"' (1961: 519–20). See also

What is Philosophy? (Deleuze and Guattari, 1994: 170) on the use of autobiography in the novel. [Tr.]

60 On faciality (*visagéité*) see 'Year Zero: Faciality' in *A Thousand Plateaus*. The celebrity or film star is a potent example of faciality at work in the cinema and on television. The use of light and shadow in the film close-up is described as 'crystallizing' (Deleuze and Guattari, 1988: 175, 168). See also 'La machine visagéitaire de Keiichi Tahara' ['Keiichi Tahara's Facialitary Machine'] in *Cartographies schizoanalytiques*, which deals extensively with 'faciality traits' in Tahara's photographic portraits. According to Guattari, Tahara is not interested in 'subjects' but in effects of subjectification. Guattari also argues that the face of Christ, as it appears on the Turin shroud, 'continues to haunt western capitalistic subjectivity' (Guattari, 1989a: 311–18). [Tr.]

61 The adjective *complexuelle* derives from the masculine noun *complexe* and refers to the psychological complex. Current in popular usage, the term has been more or less abandoned by psychoanalysis except in the specific instances of the 'Oedipus complex' and the 'castration complex'. [Tr.]

62 Part-objects are of particular importance in both Kleinian and Lacanian psychoanalysis. They are the objects towards which component instincts are directed – generally parts of the body, whether real or fantasised (breast, penis or faeces), or their symbolic equivalents. The fetish, as a substitute for the lost maternal breast, provides a clear example of an object-choice fixated upon a part object. For Lacan part-objects are those objects that 'cannot be assimilated into the subject's narcissistic illusion of completeness' (Evans, 1996: 135). The *objet petit a* introduced by Lacan differs from the Kleinian concept of the part-object in that these *objets* 'partially represent the function which produces them, and are not parts of a total unified object' (Benvenuto and Kennedy, 1986: 176–81). In *Anti-Oedipus*, Guattari and Deleuze congratulate Melanie Klein on her marvellous discovery of what they prefer to call 'partial objects', but like Lacan they are critical of her conception of their logic. Partial objects are not parts of a larger totalizing whole, such as a parental figure (breast → mother), but are non-personal and do not represent anything (1984: 42–6). Partial objects are 'the ultimate elements of the unconscious' and they operate through break-flows: 'The synthesis of connection of the partial objects is indirect, since one of the partial objects, in each point of its presence within the field, always breaks the flow that another object emits or produces relatively, itself ready to emit a flow that other partial objects will break . . . partial objects are the direct powers of the body without organs, and the body without organs, the raw material of the partial objects' (1984: 324–6). For more on the 'body without organs' see note 68. (See also Laplanche and Pontalis, 1988: 187–9; and Evans, 1996: 134–5.) [Tr.]

63 'What distinguishes metamodelization from modelization is the way it uses terms to develop possible openings onto the virtual and onto creative processuality' (Guattari, 1995a: 31). [Tr.]

64 There is a brilliant example of just such a comic redeployment of sadistic impulses in *Le Marquis*, a film by Roland Topor. [Trans: Roland Topor (1938–97), born in France of Polish origin, was a comedic everyman: a painter, cartoonist, novelist and dramatist, as well as an actor, scriptwriter and director. After studying at the Ecole des Beaux-Arts, he became involved with the journal *Bizarre* in the late 1950s, co-founding the 'Panique' movement in the early 1960s, with Fernando Arrabal (*Viva la Muerte*, 1970, Fr/Tun) and Alejandro Jodorowsky (*El Topo/The Mole*, 1971, Mex; *Santa Sangre*, 1989, It). Influenced by Dadaism and Surrealism, Topor has an irreverent and iconoclastic perspective on the world, as evidenced in *Le Marquis/Marquis*, Henri Xhonneux, 1989. In addition to *Le Marquis*, Topor wrote and co-directed with René Laloux the animated feature *La Planète Sauvage*, 1973, Czech/Fr. He also wrote the screenplay for Roman Polanski's *The Tenant/Le Locataire* (1976, Fr), adapted from Topor's own novel, *Le Locataire chimérique* (Paris: Livre de Poche, 1975). *Le Marquis* was conceived and written by Topor, who was also the film's art director. A tribute to the Marquis de Sade, it is set in the Bastille just prior to the French Revolution, with a cast described by *Time Out* as 'performing in half-animal, half-human panto drag' (Pym, 1998: 567). The Marquis de Sade himself is a droopy-eyed spaniel, whose solitary confinement is rendered somewhat less lonely by philosophic debate with his erect penis, Colin; other characters include the prison governor, a masochistic rooster and his dominant mistress/mare, Juliette; a lascivious prison guard/rat who lusts after the Marquis; and a pregnant cow, Justine, a victim of royal rape. The film charts the period 1788–89, ending on 15 July 1789, the day after the storming of the Bastille, at which point Colin and the Marquis part company – Colin to enjoy his new-found freedom with Juliette, the Marquis to continue writing. Throughout the film the Marquis has resisted Colin's physical desires, content rather to fantasize and to write; and it is no doubt for this reason that Guattari saw the film as an 'example of the comic redeployment of sadistic impulses'.]

65 Laplanche and Pontalis describe abreaction as an 'emotional discharge whereby the subject liberates himself from the affect attached to the memory of a traumatic event in such a way that this affect is not able to become (or to remain) pathogenic' (1988: 1). Essentially abreaction involves the repetition by various means – hypnotic suggestion, free association, etc. – of an originary traumatic experience, which, when repeated enables affective discharge, thus constituting a 'cure'. See also note 51 for a commentary on 'drifting away'. [Tr.]

66 See the report 'SOS Crados' in *Libération*, 17 March 1989.

67 In *A Thousand Plateaus*, the one-eyed man is the fearsome magician-emperor, a violent despot who rules by 'capture, bonds, knots and nets' over a magical-despotic State. His opposite, in terms of political sovereignty, is the wise jurist-priest-king, who legislates through treaties, pacts, alliances and laws and rules over a juridical State.

> The State apparatus is thus animated by a curious rhythm, which is first of all a great mystery: that of the Binder-Gods or magic emperors, One-Eyed men emitting from their single eye signs that capture, tie knots at a distance. The jurist-kings, on the other hand, are One-Armed men who raise their single arm as an element of right and technology, the law and the tool. In the succession of men of State, look always for the One-Eyed and the One-Armed. (1988: 424)

The irrational one-eyed man can hold everybody spellbound with his gaze, and so it seems appropriate here that Guattari is making a slighting reference to Jean-Marie Le Pen, the leader of the Front National (est. 1972), which asserts strong anti-immigration policies. [Tr.]

68 *. . . pour en finir avec les institutions pénitentiares, psychiatriques*: A wry reference to Antonin Artaud's unbroadcast 1947 radio play *Pour en finir avec le jugement de dieu* [*To Have Done with the Judgement of God*], a favourite text for Guattari and Deleuze. It was from this work that they took the idea of a 'body without organs', which Deleuze summarizes in an essay entitled 'To Have Done with Judgement': 'Artaud presents this "body without organs" that God has stolen from us in order to palm off an organized body without which his judgement could not be exercised. The body without organs is an affective, intensive, anarchist body that consists solely of poles, zones, thresholds, and gradients. It is traversed by a powerful, nonorganic vitality' (1998: 131). Artaud himself was no stranger to psychiatric institutions and he wrote his play 'primarily to denounce certain social obscenities officially sanctioned and acknowledged' (Artaud, 1988: 568). For the 'body without organs' see *Anti-Oedipus* (Deleuze and Guattari, 1984: 9–16) and 'How Do You Make Yourself a Body Without Organs?' (Deleuze and Guattari, 1988: 149–66). [Tr.]

69   One symptom of this state of affairs is the proliferation of spontaneous and co-ordinated groups (organs of 'co-ordination') wherever there are great social movements. It is notable that they often use tele-messaging to enable the expression of 'grass root' sentiments. (The Minitel 'site' 3615 + Alter is a good example of this). [Trans: Minitel is a computerized information system available via the telephone system in France. It has been available for many years and predates the popular use of the Internet.]

70   Cathexis is the English translation of the German *Besetzung*. It is a neologism created by James Strachey in the *Standard Edition*, where he also notes that Freud was unhappy with this choice. The German word is not a technical term like cathexis but is part of everyday usage; Strachey's term scientificizes Freud's discourse for a potentially sceptical English readership. Some English translators have substituted it with 'investment', a rendering that is more in keeping with economic metaphors employed by Freud in his early work. See Freud, *The Standard Edition III*: 63 n.2 and Laplanche and Pontalis (1988: 62–5). [Tr.]

71   The French word *reconversion* can also mean 'retraining'. [Tr.]

72   Deleuze's *The Fold: Leibniz and the Baroque*, published a year before *The Three Ecologies*, is an extended meditation on Leibniz's idea of an activity that 'folds, unfolds, and refolds' (*plier*, *déplier*, *replier*) matter, space and time. The act of being refolded (*replié*), to which Guattari refers here, corresponds in *The Fold* to a shrinkage of the limits in which we live and the impoverishment of our existential environment. [Tr.]

73   In *A Thousand Plateaus* one of the components of a regime of signs is diagrammatic: 'it consists in taking regimes of signs or forms of expression and extracting them from particle-signs that are no longer formalized but instead constitute unformed traits capable of combining with one another. This is the height of abstraction, but also the moment at which abstraction becomes real' (1988: 145–6)]. [Tr.]

74 In Francisco Varela's sense of the term. See *Autonomie et Connaissance*, Paris: Le Seuil, 1989. [Trans: *Autonomie et connaissance* is a revised French edition of Francisco Varela's *Principles of Biological Autonomy*. According to Varela,

> an autopoietic machine continuously generates and specifies its own organization through its operation as a system of production of its own components, and does this in an endless turnover of components under conditions of continuous perturbations and compensation of perturbations. Therefore, an autopoietic machine is a homeostatic (or rather a relations-static) system that has its own organization (defining network of relations) as the fundamental invariant . . . Every unity has an organization specifiable in terms of static or dynamic relations between elements, processes, or both. Among these possible cases, autopoietic machines are unities whose organization is defined by a particular network of processes (relations) of production of components, the autopoietic network, not by the components themselves or their static relations . . . for a machine to be autopoietic, its defining relations of production must be continuously regenerated by the components which they produce. (1979: 13)

This last point is well illustrated by Guattari when he compares jazz music to an autopoietic machine:

> Humberto Maturana and Francisco Varela proposed the concept of the autopoietic machine to define living systems. I think their notion of autopoiesis – as the auto-reproductive capacity of a structure or ecosystem – could be usefully enlarged to include social machines, economic machines and even incorporeal machines of language, theory and aesthetic creation. Jazz, for example, is simultaneously nourished by its African genealogy and by its reactualizations in multiple and heterogeneous forms. As long as it is alive it will be like that. But like any autopoietic machine, it can die for want of sustenance or drift towards destinies which make it a stranger to itself. (1995a: 93–4)

See also Varela's 'Autopoiesis: The Organization of the Living' (1973), collected in *Autopoiesis and Cognition: The Realization of the Living* (1980), co-written with Humberto R. Maturana. In his introduction, Maturana offers a useful history of the inception of the term autopoiesis:

> One day, while talking with a friend (José Bulnes) about an essay of his on Don Quixote de la Mancha, in which he analyzed Don Quixote's

dilemma of whether to follow the path of arms (*praxis*, action) or the path of letters (*poiesis*, creation, production), and his eventual choice of the path of *praxis* deferring any attempt at *poiesis*, I understood for the first time the power of the word 'poiesis' and invented the word that we needed: *autopoiesis*. This was a word without a history, a word that could directly mean what takes place in the dynamics of the autonomy proper to living systems. (xvii)

In the context of 'Living Machines', the 'autopoietic machine' is defined by Varela in the following terms:

An autopoietic machine is a machine organized (defined as a unity) as a network of processes of production (transformation and destruction) of components that produces the components which: (i) through their interactions and transformations continuously regenerate and realize the network of processes (relations) that produced them; and (ii) constitute it (the machine) as a concrete unity in the space in which they (the components) exist by specifying the topological domain of its realization as such a network. (1980: 78–9)

The living machine is specified in relation to the autopoietic machine:

If living systems are machines, that they are physical autopoietic machines is trivially obvious: they transform matter into themselves in a manner such that the product of their operation is their own organization. However we deem the converse is also true: a physical system if autopoietic, is living. In other words, we claim that the notion of *autopoiesis is necessary and sufficient to characterize the organization of living systems*. (1980: 82, italics in original)]

75 Strictly speaking the term 'mediatization' in English refers to the action of annexing a state. In French it also carries a further sense, that of immediacy. Guattari's neologistic use of the term here is, of course, clear. Note that the term connects with Guattari's concern with existential Territories. [Tr.]

76 The French word *ressourcement* refers to an upsurge or a return to basics. We have chosen the term 're-tooling' to suggest a process of renewal, although strictly speaking re-tooling has a far more specific meaning referring to the re-equipment of a factory. [Tr.].

77 On these four rapidly changing areas see Thierry Gaudin, 'Rapport sur l'état de la technique' ['Report on the state of technology'], CPE, *Science et Techniques*, special issue. [Trans: The futurologist Thierry Gaudin (*b.*

1940) has been involved in the politics of innovation and research since the early 1970s. He founded the Centre de prospective et d'évaluation, and has been an adviser to the Organisation de coopération et de développement économiques (OCDE) and the Centre national de la récherche scientifique (CNRS). He was the founder, then the President, of Fondation 2100, which became Prospective 2100, an association for studying global programmes for the next century. His books include *Les Métamorphoses du futur* (1988), *La Pensée modes d'emploi* (1989), *2100: récit du prochain siècle* (1991), *2100: Odyssée de l'espèce* (1993) and *De l'innovation* (1998).]

78 A prescient remark, anticipating the fall of the Berlin Wall in 1989 (the year in which *Les trois écologies* was published) and the eventual collapse of the USSR in December 1991, after which many of its constituent republics asserted their independence. [Tr.]

79 Gregory Bateson speaks of a 'budget of flexibility', comparing the ecological system to an acrobat on a high wire. See *Steps to an Ecology of Mind*. [Trans: Bateson defines an ecologically healthy civilization as one in which the 'flexibility' of the civilization matches that of its environment to create an open-ended 'ongoing complex system'. Flexibility here means an 'uncommitted potentiality for change'. Unfortunately, the 'man–environment system' has become increasingly unstable in parallel with man's technological advancement. Civilizations are founded on techniques for exploiting the environment (and other human beings), but they fall when they overexploit that environment. 'The new invention gives elbow room for flexibility', writes Bateson, 'but the using up of this flexibility is death.' Man needs to 'limit his greed to courses which would not destroy the ongoing total system'. To achieve 'systemic health', however, a 'high' civilization should only rely upon sustainable energy sources such as 'photosynthesis, wind, tide, and water power'. Our present civilization lacks ecological flexibility because 'people and institutions . . . have a natural propensity to eat up all available flexibility'. The ecological analyst must find ways to create flexibility in the system, while at the same time preventing it from being used up: a budget of flexibility. 'Social flexibility is a resource as precious as oil or titanium and must be budgeted in appropriate ways, to be spent . . . upon needed change.' The healthy system 'may be compared to an acrobat on a high wire. To maintain the ongoing truth of his basic premise ("I am on the wire"), he must be free to move from one position of instability to another, i.e., certain variables such as the position of his arms and the rate of movement of his arms must have great flexibility, which he uses to maintain the stability of other more fundamental and general characteristics. If his arms are fixed or paralyzed (isolated from communication), he must fall.' Rather than appeal to the law to regulate flexibility (which would only restrict the acrobat's movements and upset his balance), it should be left to 'processes of education and character formation' to change the overall ecology of ideas (1972: 495–505).]

80 As Deleuze explains in *Negotiations*, a war machine is 'nothing to do with war but to do with a particular way of occupying, taking up, space-time, or inventing new space-times: revolutionary movements . . . artistic movements too, are war machines' (1995: 172). For a full discussion of the concept see *A Thousand Plateaus* (Deleuze and Guattari, 1988: 351–423). [Tr.]

81 Walter Benjamin, *Illuminations*, trans. by Harry Zohn, ed. by Hannah Arendt (London: Fontana, 1992 [1973]). [Trans: The first two sentences that Guattari cites do not appear in the Fontana translation, and are taken from Chris Turner's abridged translation of *Les trois écologies* (Guattari, 1989d: 147)].

82 A *chape* is a cope, a long cloak-like vestment worn by a priest or bishop in ceremonies and processions. The word derives from the medieval Latin *capella*, as does the English word 'chapel'. Like Nietzsche, Guattari regards Christianity as a great step backwards for humankind (see Guattari 1984: 180). On the psychology of the priest, see *Anti-Oedipus* (Deleuze and Guattari, 1984: 269, 332). A neuroleptic is generally any antipsychotic drug used in the treatment of psychoses, particularly schizophrenia. These drugs have a tranquilizing effect, and produce in the patient a general quietude, a slowing of responsiveness to external stimuli and a lessening of attentiveness. [Tr.]

83 As far as 'global ecology' is concerned, Jacques Robin, in a report entitled *Penser à la fois l'écologie, la société et l'Europe* ['Reflections on Ecology, Society and Europe'], addresses with a rare competence and along similar lines to my own, the links between scientific ecology and economic ecology and the emergence of their ethical implications. (*Groupe Ecologie d'Europe 93* [The European Ecology Group 93], 22, rue Dussoubs, 75002 Paris, 1989.)

The Life and Work of Félix Guattari: From Transversality to Ecosophy

1 Others have suggested much the same of Guattari in his heyday (Turkle, 1980; Genosko, 1998b: 107–8). Indeed, Guattari himself was deeply troubled as an analyst of the Ecole freudienne of his position as 'Guru Despite Himself' (Guattari, 1995b: 11).

2 It is useful to put into relief Guattari's early suspicions about the politics of transference, which he lived through during his training under Lacan, in terms of a recently published conversation on this topic he had in 1989 with the Israeli analyst Bracha Lichtenberg-Ettinger (Guattari, 1997: 613): 'In my work I do not focus on transference. My role consists in helping the patient develop means of expression and processes of subjectification that would not exist with the analytic process. Often transference is nothing more than opposition to the analysis, which Lacanians tend to use manipulatively.' Orthodox analysts would dismissively claim that Guattari is simply not engaging in analysis since he eschews transference in his individual practice as well as in his institutional work at La Borde. Manipulation is tied to typical analytic cries of 'resistance'! This is how analysts protect their honour, Guattari remarked; the question of the so-called 'negative transference', which Freud described as the clouding over of the fair skies of the treatment, puts the blame on the patient for a change in the weather, rather than leading to a self-questioning by the analyst about why the treatment is going nowhere; it is also a typical reason given to go on interminably – oh, the negative transference, well, it's business as usual!

3 I first developed the concept of the bestiary of theory in relation to classic psychoanalytic texts (Genosko, 1993: 602–32; 1994: 1–31). My goal was to reveal the 'moral' tales – the pillars and remarkable caninophilia of the Freudian bestiary – told by the reproduction of animals found therein, as well as in the professional and domestic lives of analysts such as Freud, Ernest Jones and Marie Bonaparte. I later (Guattari, 1996b: 1–34; Genosko, 1998a: 529–42) turned my attention to Deleuze and Guattari, suggesting, somewhat schematically, that the psycho- and schizoanalytic bestiaries of Freud and Guattari overlap on the matter of how they do things with horses and porcupines. I was inspired by the extraordinarily insightful and provocative plateau 2 of Deleuze and

Guattari's *A Thousand Plateaus* on Freud's case of the Wolf-Man.
It seemed to me that they showed for the first time how productive
the close scrutiny of the animal life of a text could be. Subsequently,
scenes of animal reproduction became for me a way of reading Deleuze
and Guattari's own writings; a way, then, of tracking their arguments
across the plateaux by means of signs left by the animals of their own
theoretical bestiary. While this sounds remarkably simple – as simple
as following fresh tracks – it takes practice, as any naturalist would
admit – even a bad bird watcher like Freud – and a firm grasp of the
identifying features of the species at issue. Even a textual bestiary makes
demands on animal fanciers. Initially, I had some trouble distinguishing
the true lobsters of plateau 3 from the spiny lobsters of 11 in *A Thousand
Plateaus*. Contextual or field conditions are not, of course, the main
concern, nor is it a question of mastering a scientific literature; rather, the
bestiarist is called upon to track these creatures as they perform varied
theoretical work and to bring to bear a certain amount of background
knowledge, in the manner of a naturalist, upon the discussion of
the services performed. The animal life of texts is one of the three
preoccupations of what I have elsewhere dubbed undisciplined theorizing
(Genosko, 1998c).

4   One may be wondering about what becomes of the superego in the
period of *Anti-Oedipus*? One of earliest reviews of *Anti-Oedipus* that
appeared in English pointed out with surprise that:

> Of all the objections made to recent psychoanalytic gospels, none
> is stranger and more saddening than that which urgently warns us
> against the perils of having a psyche without a superego. One would
> have thought that Necessity, or the interplay of individuals with the
> 'machines' of the world, was sufficient superego on its own, without
> having to cope with internal restrictions almost invariably born of fear
> or envy. (Anonymous, 1973: 296)

It's true: Deleuze and Guattari were constantly looking over their shoulders
for traces of superegos; and they found all sorts of superegos (that of
literature, of art . . .). The fact that they kept looking was evidence enough
that one didn't just discard the superego. The mutual derivations of
subjugated and subject groups tells us a great deal about the survival of
the superego because the former is perfused with 'the mechanisms for
the repression of desire', and the strong superego of this hierarchized
group is constrasted with the non-hierarchized latter group which
apparently has no superego; instead, the subject group 'opposes real

coefficients of transversality to symbolic determinations of subjugation' (Deleuze and Guattari, 1977: 349). The non-absolute distinction between the two kinds of groups requires one to uphold the superego. Looking backwards at the surrealist group, Deleuze and Guattari see the superego named Breton, whom they contrast with Artaud-the-Schizo; still, they admitted that 'there will always be a Breton against Artaud' (1977: 134). There will always be, in other words, a superego. Even the most revolutionary subject groups will run up against one.

Bibliography

Anonymous (1973) 'In the Factory of the Unconscious', *TLS* (16 March): 295–6.

Armitage, John (1997) 'Accelerated Aesthetics: Paul Virilio's *The Vision Machine*', *Angelaki* 2/3: 199–209.

Artaud, Antonin (1988) *Selected Writings*, ed. Susan Sontag, Berkeley: University of California Press.

Baker, Phil (2000) *Secret City*, London: Free Association.

Bateson, Gregory (1972) *Steps to an Ecology of Mind*, New York: Ballantine.

Baudrillard, Jean (1995) *The Gulf War Did Not Take Place*, trans. by Paul Patton, Sydney: Power Publications.

Beckett, Samuel, *et al.* (1972 [1929]) *Our Exagmination Round His Factification for Incamination of Work in Progress*, London: Faber and Faber.

Benjamin, Walter (1992 [1973]) *Illuminations*, trans. by Harry Zohn, ed. by Hannah Arendt, London: Fontana.

Benn, Maurice B. (1976) *The Drama of Revolt: A Critical Study of Georg Büchner*, Cambridge: Cambridge University Press.

Benvenuto, Bice and Kennedy, Roger (1986) *The Works of Jacques Lacan: An Introduction*, London: Free Association.

Bergson, Henri (1928) *Creative Evolution*, trans. by Arthur Mitchell, London: Macmillan.

Blanchot, Maurice (1993) *The Infinite Conversation*, trans. by Susan Hanson, Minneapolis: University of Minnesota Press.

Bombard, Alain (1979) *Histoire du naufragé volontaire*, Paris: F. Nathan.

Bosteels, Bruno (1998) 'From Text to Territory: Félix Guattari's Cartographies of the Unconscious', in *Deleuze and Guattari: New Mappings in Politics, Philosophy, and Culture*, ed. by Eleanor Kaufman and Kevin Jon Heller, Minneapolis: University of Minnesota Press.

Boundas, Constantin (1993) 'Foreclosure of the Other: From Sartre to Deleuze', *Journal of the British Society for Phenomenology* 24/1 (Jan.).

Braudel, Fernand (1973) *Capitalism and Material Life 1400–1800*, trans. by
    Miriam Kochan, London: Weidenfeld & Nicolson.
Carter, Alan (1999) *A Radical Green Political Theory*, London: Routledge.
Chapman, Graham, *et al*. (1997) *Environmentalism and the Mass Media:
    The North–South Divide*, London: Routledge.
Conley, Verena Andermatt (1997) *Ecopolitics: The Environment in Post-
    structuralist Thought*, London: Routledge.
Cummins, Jim and Sayers, Dennis (1995) *Brave New Schools: Challenging
    Cultural Illiteracy through Global Learning Networks*, London: Macmillan.
Deleuze, Gilles (1972) *Proust and Signs*, trans. by Richard Howard, New York:
    Braziller.
— (1981) *Francis Bacon: Logique de la sensation*, Paris: Différence.
— (1986) *Cinema I: The Movement Image*, trans. by Hugh Tomlinson and
    Barbara Habberjam, London: The Athlone Press.
— (1989) *Cinema 2: The Time-Image*, trans. by Hugh Tomlinson and Robert
    Galeta, London: The Athlone Press.
— (1990) *The Logic of Sense*, trans. by Mark Lester, New York: Columbia
    University Press.
— (1993) *The Fold: Leibniz and the Baroque*, trans. by Tom Conley, London:
    The Athlone Press.
— (1994) *Difference and Repetition*, trans. by Paul Patton, London: The
    Athlone Press.
— (1995) *Negotiations: 1972–1990*, trans. by Martin Joughin, New York:
    Columbia University Press.
— (1998) *Essays Critical and Clinical*, trans. by Daniel W. Smith and Michael A.
    Greco, London: Verso.
Deleuze, Gilles and Guattari, Félix (1984) *Anti-Oedipus: Capitalism and
    Schizophrenia I*, trans. by Robert Hurley, Mark Seem and Helen R. Lane,
    London: The Athlone Press.
— (1986) *Kafka: Toward a Minor Literature*, trans. by Dana Polan, Minneapolis:
    University of Minnesota Press.
— (1988) *A Thousand Plateaus: Capitalism and Schizophrenia II*, trans. by
    Brian Massumi, London: The Athlone Press
— (1994) *What is Philosophy?*, trans. by Hugh Tomlinson and Graham
    Burchell, New York: Columbia University Press.
Deleuze, Gilles and Parnet, Claire (1987) *Dialogues*, trans. by Hugh Tomlinson
    and Barbara Habberjam, New York: Columbia University Press.
Deleuze, Gilles and Sacher-Masoch, Leopold von (1989) *Masochism*, New
    York: Zone Books.

Depussé, Marie (1993) *Dieu gît dans les détails: La Borde un asile*, Paris: P.O.L.

Doyle, Sir Arthur Conan (1952 [1912/13]) *The Professor Challenger Stories*, John Murray: London.

Dufresne, Todd (2000) *Tales from the Freudian Crypt*, Stanford: Stanford University Press

Evans, Dylan (1996) *An Introductory Dictionary of Lacanian Psychoanalysis*, London: Routledge.

Freud, Sigmund (1953–74) *The Standard Edition of the Complete Psychological Works of Sigmund Freud* (24 vols), London: Hogarth Press and the Institute of Psychoanalysis.

— *Early Psycho-Analytic Publications*, *SE* 3.

— *The Unconscious*, *SE* 14.

— *Group Psychology and the Analysis of the Ego*, *SE* 18.

— *The Ego and the Id*, *SE* 19.

— *New Introductory Lectures on Psychoanalysis*, *SE* 22.

— *Analysis Terminable and Interminable*, *SE* 23.

— (1983) *New Introductory Lectures on Psychoanalysis*, trans. by James Strachey, ed. by James Strachey and Angela Richards, London: Penguin.

— (1984) *On Metapsychology: The Theory of Psychoanalysis*, trans. by James Strachey, ed. by Angela Richards, London: Penguin.

Gallop, Jane (1985) *Reading Lacan*, Ithaca: Cornell University Press.

Genosko, Gary (1993) 'Freud's Bestiary: How Does Psychoanalysis Treat Animals?' *The Psychoanalytic Review* 80/4.

— (1994) 'Introduction', Marie Bonaparte, *Topsy*, New Brunswick: Transaction.

— (1998a) 'A Bestiary of Territoriality and Expression: Poster Fish, Bower Birds and Spiny Lobsters', *Canadian Review of Comparative Literature* 24/3.

— (1998b) 'Guattari's Schizoanalytic Semiotics: Mixing Hjelmslev and Pierce', in *Deleuze and Guattari: New Mappings in Politics*, *Philosophy*, *and Culture*, ed. by Eleanor Kaufman and Kevin Jon Heller, Minneapolis: University of Minnesota Press.

— (1998c) *Undisciplined Theory*, London: Sage.

Goodchild, Philip (1996) *Deleuze and Guattari: An Introduction to the Politics of Desire*, London: Sage.

Guattari, Félix (1972) *Psychanalyse et transversalité: essais d'analyse institutionelle*, Paris: François Maspero.

— (1977) *La révolution moléculaire*, Fontenay-sous-Bois: Éditions Recherches.

— (1979) *L'inconscient machinique: essais de schizo-analyse*, Fontenay-sous-Bois: Éditions Recherches.

— (1984) *Molecular Revolution: Psychiatry and Politics*, trans. by Rosemary Sheed, London: Penguin.

— (1986) *Les années d'hiver 1980–1985*, Paris: Barrault.

— (1989a) *Cartographies schizoanalytiques*, Paris: Éditions Galilée.

— (1989b) *Les trois écologies*, Paris: Galilée.

— (1989c) 'Une révolution moléculaire: entretien avec Félix Guattari', in *La Revue Autrement: L'Esprit des drogues*, série Mutations No. 106, Paris: Autrement.

— (1989d) 'The Three Ecologies', trans. by Chris Turner, Material Word, *New Formations* 8: 131–47.

— (1992) *Chaosmose*, Paris: Galilée.

— (1995a) *Chaosmosis: an Ethico–aesthetic Paradigm*, trans. by Paul Bains and Julian Pefanis, Sydney: Power Publications.

— (1995b) *Chaosophy*, trans. by Charles Wolff, New York: Semiotext(e).

— (1996a) *Soft Subversions*, trans. by David L. Sweet and Chet Weiner, ed. by Sylvère Lotringer, New York: Semiotext(e).

— (1996b) *The Guattari Reader*, ed. by Gary Genosko, Oxford: Basil Blackwell.

— (1997) 'From Transference to the Aesthetic Paradigm: Interview with Bracha Lichtenberg-Ettinger', *Canadian Review of Comparative Literature* 24/3: 611–21.

Guattari, Félix and Negri, Toni (1990) *Communists Like Us: New Spaces of Liberty, New Lines of Alliance*, trans. by Michael Ryan, New York: Semiotext(e).

Hardy, Thomas (1987 [1886]) *The Mayor of Casterbridge*, London: Penguin Books.

Holland, Eugene (1988) 'The Ideology of Lack in Lackanianism', in *Ethics/Aesthetics: Post-Modern Positions*, ed. by Robert Merill, pp. 59–69.

Joyce, James (1960 [1939]) *Finnegans Wake*, London: Faber and Faber.

— (1986 [1922]) *Ulysses*, London: Penguin Books.

Kafka, Franz (1987 [1925]) *The Trial*, trans. Willa and Edwin Muir, ed. by Max Brod, London: Penguin.

Klein, Melanie (1950 [1934]) 'A Contribution to the Psychogenesis of Manic-Depressive States', in *Contributions to Psychoanalysis*, London: Hogarth.

Lacan, Jacques (1977) *Ecrits: A Selection*, trans. by Alan Sheridan, New York: W. W. Norton.

— (1987 [1979]) *The Four Fundamental Concepts of Psychoanalysis*, trans. by Alan Sheridan, London: Penguin.

— (1991 [1968]) *Speech and Language in Psychoanalysis*, trans. by Anthony Wilden, Baltimore and London: Johns Hopkins University Press.

— (1993) *The Seminar of Jacques Lacan: Book III 1955–1956: The Psychoses*, ed. by Jacques-Alain Miller, trans. by Russell Grigg, New York and London: Routledge.

Lacoue-Labarthe, Philippe and Nancy, Jean-Luc (1978) *L'Absolu littéraire: théorie de la littérature du romantisme allemand*, Paris: Èditions de Seuil.

Laplanche, Jean and Pontalis, Jean-Bertrand (1988) *The Language of Psychoanalysis*, London: Karnac and the Institute of Psychoanalysis.

Lawrence, D. H. (1961) *Phoenix: The Posthumous Papers of D. H. Lawrence*, London: Heinemann.

Leslie, John (1998) *The End of the World: The Science and Ethics of Human Extinction*, London: Routledge.

Litt, Toby (1997) *Adventures in Capitalism*, London: Minerva.

Lyotard, Jean-François (1984) *Driftworks*, New York: Semiotext(e).

Marx, Karl (1973) *Grundrisse*, trans. Martin Nicolaus, New York: Vintage.

Massumi, Brian (1988) 'Deleuze and Guattari's Theories of the Group Subject, Through a Reading of Corneille's *Le Cid*', *Discours social/Social Discourse* 1/4: 423–40.

Nietzsche, Friedrich (1968) *The Will to Power*, trans. by Walter Kaufmann and R. J. Hollingdale, New York: Random House.

Oury, Jean *et al.* (1977) 'La Borde: un lieu psychiatrique pas comme les autres', *La Quinzaine littéraire* 250: 20–1.

Pascal, Blaise (1995) *Pensées and Other Writings*, trans. by Honor Levi, Oxford: Oxford University Press.

Plant, Sadie (1992) *The Most Radical Gesture: The Situationist International in a Postmodern Age*, London: Routledge.

Prigogine, Ilya and Stengers, Isabelle (1985) *Order Out of Chaos*, London: HarperCollins.

— (1988) *Entre le temps et l'éternité*, Paris: Fayard.

Proust, Marcel (1996 [1913]) *In Search of Lost Time*, Vol. I: *Swann's Way*, trans. by C. K. Scott Moncrieff and Terence Kilmartin, London: Vintage.

Pym, John, ed. (1998) *Time Out Film Guide*, London: Penguin.

Ragland-Sullivan, Ellie (1991) 'The Sexual Masquerade: A Lacanian Theory of Sexual Difference', in *Lacan and the Subject of Language*, New York: Routledge, pp. 49–80.

Rees, Martin (1997) *Before the Beginning: Our Universe and Others*, London: Simon & Schuster.

Reich, Wilhelm (1975 [1946]) *The Mass Psychology of Fascism*, trans. by Vincent R. Carfagno, Harmondsworth: Pelican.

Sartre, Jean-Paul (1976) *Critique of Dialectical Reason*, vol. 1, trans. by Alan Sheridan-Smith, London: NLB.

Stivale, Charles (1985) 'Pragmatic/Machinic: Discussion with Félix Guattari', http://www.dc.peachnet.edu/'mnunes/guattari.html.

Suliman, Mohamed, ed. (1999) *Ecology, Politics and Violent Conflict*, London: Zen Books.

Sylvester, David (1987) *The Brutality of Fact: Interviews with Francis Bacon*, London: Thames & Hudson.

Topor, Roland (1975) *Le Locataire chimérique*, Paris: Livre de Poche.

Turkle, Sherry (1980) 'French Anti-Psychiatry', in *Critical Psychiatry*, ed. by David Ingleby, New York: Pantheon, pp. 150–83.

Varela, Francisco (1973) 'Autopoiesis: The Organization of the Living', in Francisco Varela and Humberto R. Mutarana (1980) *Autopoiesis and Cognition: The Realization of the Living*, Dordrecht and London: Reidel.

— (1979) *Principles of Biological Autonomy*, New York and Oxford: North Holland.

— (1989) *Autonomie et Connaissance*, Paris: Le Seuil.

Virilio, Paul (1986) *Speed and Politics: An Essay on Dromology*, New York: Semiotext(e).

— (1989) *War and Cinema: The Logisitics of Perception*, trans. by Patrick Camiller, London: Verso.

— (1991) *The Aesthetics of Disappearance*, trans. by Philip Beitchman, New York: Semiotext(e).

— (1994) *The Vision Machine*, trans. by Julie Rose, London and Indiana: BFI and Indiana University Press.

Warhol, Andy (1989) *The Andy Warhol Diaries*, New York: Warner.

Wilden, Anthony (1991 [1968]) 'Lacan and the Discourse of the Other', in Jacques Lacan, *Speech and Language in Psychoanalysis*, trans. by Anthony Wilden, Baltimore and London: Johns Hopkins University Press.

Winnicott, D. W. (1971) *Playing and Reality*, New York: Basic Books.

— (1994 [1991]) *Playing and Reality*, London and New York: Routledge.

Index